Constructing Buildings, Bridges, and Minds

Constructing Buildings, Bridges, and Minds

Building an Integrated Curriculum
Through Social Studies

Katherine A. Young

Boise State University

HEINEMANN
Portsmouth, NH

HEINEMANN
A Division of Reed Publishing (USA) Inc.
361 Hanover Street   Portsmouth, NH   03801-3912
Offices and agents throughout the world

Editor: Dawn Boyer   Text design: George McLean
Production: Melissa L. Inglis   Cover Design: Joni Doherty

Every effort has been made to contact the copyright holders for permission to reprint borrowed material where necessary. We regret any oversights that may have occurred and would be happy to rectify them in future printings of this work.

Library of Congress Cataloging-in-Publication Data
Young, Katherine A.
   Constructing buildings, bridges, and minds : building an
integrated curriculum through social studies / Katherine A. Young.
     p.   cm.
   Includes bibliographical references and index.
   ISBN 0-435-08796-7
   1. Social sciences—Study and teaching (Elementary)—United
States.   2. Active learning—United States.   3. Curriculum planning—
United States.   4. Education, Elementary—Activity programs—United
States.   I. Title.
LB1584.Y68   1993
372.83'043—dc20   93-28835
                                           CIP

Printed in the United States of America on acid-free paper.
99 98 97 96 95 94 93   CC   1 2 3 4 5 6 7

Contents

Preface

A Classroom Adventure

You are about to embark on a most unusual classroom adventure. Soon you will be introduced to the culminating activity of a major classroom project that integrates several strands of the elementary/middle school curriculum. The scene is active and often noisy. Children scramble everywhere, while assorted adults tour a classroom that has no desks or chairs but which is nearly filled by a sprawling model—Washington, DC, in the fifth grade; Latin America in the sixth grade.

At first you may mistake the activity for confusion, and you may question whether worthwhile learning is taking place. I hope that by the time you finish the adventure you will be convinced that this process is the best possible way to teach. It can be used at any grade level: fourth graders can build their state, primary children can build their neighborhood or community, and more mature students can build continents, nations, cities, or governments. This framework is suitable for elementary, middle school, junior high school, and high school students. Teachers at any level can develop their own projects based on their own curricula and their own students' interests.

Why do I teach the way I do? Why did I develop this way of learning for students? Why does this way of teaching keep calling to me? This is not the stuff of linear steps to learning, and it is definitely not a prepackaged foolproof linear model. Maybe I am attracted to this pattern of "whole learning" precisely because it is non-linear.

I don't learn much in a linear fashion. I need a good tangent now and then, or some dabbling, and then, to counteract that, a little something in depth. Along the way, questions intrude, too, making my thinking even messier. I find the thrill of a cognitive risk—a testing of ideas—to be exhilarating.

Do we really learn by memorizing little bits and pieces, minute facts in a sequential order, and then miraculously produce a complex synthesis? At some point, I stumbled onto the idea that all learning is interrelated. I will boldly state that much learning is not linear. Learning is not one workbook page after another, or one worksheet after another.

For my first two weeks as a fifth-grade teacher, I dutifully followed the reductionist's plan. We looked at each word and task with a microscope and ended up not knowing for sure what we had accomplished. It is small wonder that students often complain that their education lacks relevance.

The following story may illustrate my point. A friend of mine, at the age of seventy, jumped from a plane that crashed at take-off. Fortunately she survived, and her subsequent experiences reminded me of my first few weeks of teaching. She told of having a back doctor, eye doctor, foot doctor, ear doctor, internist, and surgeon. None of these doctors communicated with the others about the ear or foot or eye or whatever the part was. Each just treated one small part, and understandably, my friend didn't respond well. "I'd like be treated like a whole person, not just a collection of unrelated parts," she complained.

That's how I treated the subjects my fifth graders were studying during my first two weeks of teaching. We looked at one subject and then another as if there were no relationship. Neither the students nor I responded well to studying assorted bits and pieces.

After two boring weeks I made changes. When I say boring, I'm speaking from my viewpoint. And, if it is boring for the teacher, try to imagine how deadening it must be for the students. I wonder now if, perhaps by chance, I had a classroom of learners who, like myself, were non-linear. A rarity? Not at all. Each year I have had students who mainly thrived on knowledge generated by activities that developed personal understanding.

It is obvious to me now that I began integrating curriculum before it became fashionable. During the third week of teaching, I started integrating all of the subject areas using some kind of theme or project to carry them along. That first year was a series of unsophisticated efforts. As teachers, we tend to improve with experience, however. Each year, as we learn more about children and how they learn, we become more adept. *Constructing Buildings, Bridges, and Minds* is the product of many years of experience—trial and error, experimentation, refinement, and increasing sophistication—in the integration of curriculum.

I must warn you that this book contains no six-step plans or cute recipes for integrated teaching and learning. In fact, this kind of education cannot be reduced to formula. My kind of integrated curriculum is free-flowing, flexible, and frequently spontaneous—quite the antithesis of formula teaching. Still, the process is not without guidelines, expectations, and accountability. It is essential for you, the teacher, to set guidelines and expectations that seem appropriate and reasonable for your classroom. Once you have done this, it is off to a great adventure!

As you read *Constructing Buildings, Bridges, and Minds*, you will hear me speak from two perspectives: the classroom teacher and the professor. I was the elementary teacher for twenty years; I am the professor now. I know that integration works, because I was there in the public school classroom—I used it and saw the results. Now as a professor I understand *why* it works, for I have since learned many of the theoretical bases that explain its success. It is my hope that my two perspectives—integrated, if you like—produce a synthesis that is reasonable and useful as we all explore the workings of the integrated classroom.

Although I have many rational, logical arguments for using this kind of integrated curriculum, I must admit that there is an emotional side as well. I have enjoyed many emotional rewards over the years, but none more powerful than Donald's story. Whenever I question this method of teaching, I think of Donald and know that for me this is the only way I can ever teach.

Donald's Story

To be fair to each student and avoid my own biases, when the project begins I always put the names of buildings in a hat and let the students draw for their buildings. One year Donald reached in the hat and pulled out the Capitol building. If I had chosen the student least likely to construct the Capitol, it would have been Donald. Inwardly I got queasy. But what could I do? If we traded, I might just as well announce that Donald would not be able to do the kind of work I wanted on the Capitol. Instead, I got hold of myself and thought, "Look, maybe he can do it, and if not, at least he had a chance. I'll help him if he wants any help. So what if the Capitol looks different this year. After all, this is a project for kids."

So, Donald kept the Capitol and was very excited. A few days later, his mom came to school and asked if he could work on the Capitol at home with his dad. My policy allows students to work on their projects at school, so that they don't have to work on them at home. However, I feel that when parents *want* to work with their child at home, that's great. In fact, many parents do get involved with their child's project.

Well, Donald often reported that he and Dad were working on the Capitol out in the garage. Because his own building was at home, Donald became involved with helping several of the other students whose projects were at school. Since he had always been a poor student and unmotivated, I was happy to see him getting interested.

Later his mom called to tell me that Donald and his dad were often out in the garage until midnight working on the Capitol. She added, "That's why Donald won't have his homework in today. Is that okay?" What could I say?

When Donald walked in with the Capitol, it was beautiful! We all loved it, and told Donald so in many ways. We found the right spot on the floor for it, and Donald's Capitol was an inspiration to all of us.

Shortly thereafter, I had parent conferences. Donald's mom and dad both came in—something that Dad had never done before. Both parents sat and cried as they told me how previously Donald and his dad had never gotten along with each other, but that creating the Capitol had brought them very close together. While they were also happy that Donald had learned so much, that paled when they realized what had happened to their relationships.

This is a wonderful story, but it doesn't stop there. Years later, a colleague came to see me with news about Donald. She had been shopping at the grocery store when she ran into Donald, his wife, and baby. The Capitol project popped up in their conversation, and Donald, who is now a truck driver, said that the Capitol was sitting proudly on their TV in the living room. The Capitol, he said, had changed his life.

What if I had been foolish and given that building to a child who I *knew* could do it?

I will always believe in this kind of teaching. And so will Donald.

Acknowledgments

I am forever indebted to all those wonderful students without whom there would have been no book. A special debt is owed to those who took the time and effort to write about their project experiences and to share their picture albums. Each and every one of my students throughout the years has contributed to the experiences and understandings put forth here.

A note of special appreciation and thanks is owed to the parents and other volunteers who invested countless hours and days of their time to work with the children. Special thanks go to those who put their memories and feelings on paper in support of this book.

I have been grateful indeed for the many colleagues who have put up with the noise, confusion, and clutter generated each year by the projects. Over the years they have given me support, encouragement, and assistance. Thanks gang!

Nothing important can ever succeed at a school without the blessing and help of the office and custodial staff. The secretaries must have fielded thousands of calls and sent as many messages for me and the students. Likewise, the custodians patiently and cheerfully cleaned up hundreds of messes and accidents, helped children find building materials, and encouraged them in their construction. Some years, the secretary and/or the custodian would come in after school each day and critique the day's work. What terrific people!

I owe special thanks to the fine Boise administrators who supported my efforts during these projects: Leona Burkett and Bob Wecker, principals of Campus Elementary School; Arvin Spofford, principal of Liberty Elementary School; Dr. Richard Kuntz, Director of Elementary Education; and Dr. Barney Parker, Superintendent of Schools. Dick Kuntz and Barney Parker were in my classroom many times, and my principals were involved on an almost daily basis.

Last but not least is my appreciation and thanks for a wonderful family. My husband, Virgil, and daughter, Susie, were always there to lend their hearts and hands when needed.

Introduction: Messing Around—And Other Connections to Learning

What you do every day, after all, is what forms your mind.

— Bill McKibben, *The Age of Missing Information*

If we don't stimulate children's minds—strengthen those neurons and synapses—they only develop footpaths of knowledge, with weeds growing everywhere. It's our job as educators to turn those footpaths into superhighways.

— Terrel Bell, former U. S. Secretary of Education

*W*riting this book has prompted me to think a great deal about the process of learning, and I have also learned a great deal by writing it. As an elementary teacher, I intuitively knew that children learned more when they put ideas on paper. Now from massive personal exposure, I can attest to the efficacy of "writing to learn," which I advocate in this book.

I did not approach writing this book as a theorist, but as a teacher whose life has been spent in the classroom where the real action takes place. What I have learned is based on real interactions with real kids. On the other hand, it is necessary to understand some theory in order to know the "why behind the how." How else will we be able to apply the appropriate strategy in the classroom at the appropriate time? I have never been able to make six-step plans work for me, because they tend to be so inflexible. However, such plans are unnecessary—and sometimes silly—when we understand the theory relating to what we are trying to accomplish.

Much of what I learned deals with understanding the interaction of theory and practice, validating my teaching strategies, and discovering a new vocabulary for the not-so-new tried-and-true. I was already familiar with John Dewey's "learning by doing," but the ramifications of "experiential learning" were rather nebulous until I was compelled to explore them while writing. Though it does not sound very scholarly, the term "messing around" is highly descriptive of some kinds of experiential learning.

Messing Around

Anthropologist Claude Levi-Strauss observed that people of primitive cultures "mess around" with things in the process of learning. He is credited with coining the word *bricoleur* to describe someone who does this: "a kind of intuitive technician who plays with concepts and objects in order to learn about them" (Rheingold 1988, 90). Doesn't this also sound a little like the behavior that our culture associates with genius, and which many educators work to encourage in their students? Doesn't this also sound a bit like project learning?

In our modern, sanitized world, children have relatively few constructive opportunities to "mess around." However, nearly all children love to tinker and explore. A young child may take a toy apart to see how it is made, or pull out pots and pans from under the kitchen counter (during an unguarded moment). An older child may be found experimenting with cooking, whittling, bicycling, hiking, or perhaps with a puzzle or something intriguing found in a book. Three notable people of our time were definitely *bricoleurs:* Seymour Papert, Richard Feynman, and Annie Dillard. Their stories are instructive.

Turning wheels in his head   As a very young child, Seymour Papert became fascinated with automobiles, and much of his early vocabulary came from his knowledge of automobiles. "I was particularly proud of knowing about the parts of the transmission system, the gearbox, and most especially the differential"

(Papert 1980, vi). In his book *Mindstorms*, Papert describes how his "messing" with gears created paradigms for organizing other ideas that he encountered, especially those in mathematics:

> It was, of course, many years later before I understood how the gears work; but once I did, playing with gears became a favorite pastime. I loved rotating circular objects against one another in gearlike motions. . . . I became adept at turning wheels in my head and making chains of cause and effect. . . . I found particular pleasure in such systems as the differential gear, which does not follow a simple linear chain of causality since the motion of the transmission can be distributed in many different ways to the two wheels depending on what resistance they encounter. . . . I believe that working with differentials did more for my mathematical development than anything I was taught in elementary school. (vi)

Later in life, Seymour Papert invented LOGO, a computer language that enables children to program computers and explore mathematical concepts in physical ways. If you understand LOGO, you can see its connection to the boy who turned wheels in his head.

"He fixes radios by thinking" As a child and as an adult, Richard Feynman pursued his immense curiosity about how things work, and he was forever "messing around." When he was eleven or twelve years old, he set up a lab in his house, where he began messing around with electricity—building circuits, fuses, and voltage adapters. He was also fascinated by radios. He relates:

> I enjoyed radios. I started with a crystal set that I bought at the store, and I used to listen to it at night in bed while I was going to sleep. . . . I bought radios at rummage sales. I didn't have any money, but . . . they were old, broken radios, and I'd buy them and try to fix them.
>
> Usually they were broken in some simple-minded way . . . so I could get some of them going. . . . it was tremendously exciting!" (Feynman 1985, 3-5)

Eventually, the manager of a hotel called Feynman to repair some radios, even though Feynman was just a boy. "The main reason people hired me was the Depression," Feynman said. "They didn't have any money to fix their radios, and they'd heard about this kid who would do it for less" (7). Most of the repair jobs were simple, he said, but they became increasingly more difficult. One job in particular was memorable.

Young Feynman was called to repair a radio that made a tremendous amount of noise when turned on, but quieted down to normal after it warmed up. He tells the story as follows:

> So I started to think: "How can that happen?" I began walking back and forth, thinking, and I realized that one way it can happen is that the tubes are heating up in the wrong order—that is, the amplifier's all hot, the tubes are ready to go, and there's nothing feeding in, or there's some back circuit feeding in, or. . . . So the guy says, "What are you doing? You come to fix the radio, and you're only walking back and forth!" I say, "I'm thinking!" Then I said to myself, "All right, take the tubes out, and reverse the order completely in the set". . . . So I changed the tubes around, stepped to the front of the radio, turned the thing on, and it's as quiet as a lamb: it waits until it heats up, then plays perfectly—no noise. (7-8)

Later, the owner of the radio spread the word of young Feynman's talent, marveling, "He fixes radios by thinking!" (8).

Richard Feynman became one of the world's greatest physicists and won the Nobel prize in physics in 1965. Later, it was Feynman who discovered (by thinking) that faulty rubber O-rings were the cause of the infamous 1986 space shuttle *Challenger* disaster that resulted in the deaths of seven astronauts.

Pushing at her map's edges   As soon as Annie Dillard could say her phone number, her mother let her explore the neighborhood alone. Annie was seven years old. As she walked, she "memorized the neighborhood." "I made a mental map and located myself on it," she wrote. "At night in bed I rehearsed the small world's scheme and set challenges. Find the store using backyards only. Imagine a route from the school to my friend's house" (Dillard 1987, 42).

Annie rode her bicycle "over the world's known edge," as she expressed it. She discovered the football field beyond the school, and

Frick Park, where her father forbid her to go. He said it was dangerous, but she went anyway. Annie got a bird book and wandered the deep woods to study the woodpeckers, cardinals, and robins, not to mention the squirrels and chipmunks. She never met any people in the park except one woman who walked her dachshunds there.

> [In the winter, I] searched for panther tracks in the snow. In summer and fall I imagined the woods extending infinitely. I was the first human to see these shadowed trees, this land; I would make my pioneer clearing here, near the water. . . .
>
> Walking was my project before reading. The text I read was the town; the book I made up was a map. First I walked across one of our side yards to the blackened alley. . . . Now I walked to piano lessons, four long blocks north of school and three zigzag blocks into an Irish neighborhood near Thomas Boulevard. I pushed at my map's edges. . . . (43-44)

These experiences in childhood impressed themselves on Annie's consciousness, filling her mind with images and experiences, challenging her intellect, stimulating her creativity, molding her future. Today Annie Dillard, author of *Pilgrim at Tinker Creek,* is one of America's major writers.

Preparing Students to Compose Their Lives

Mary Catherine Bateson, in her book, *Composing a Life,* explores the lives of five contemporary American women. These were successful, high-achieving women who lived complex lives. From her study, Bateson concluded that successful lives are not one-dimensional, and that the road to high achievement requires learning to integrate many activities and facets of life at one time. Life requires what she calls multiplicity of learning:

> There are tasks that really do require extended narrow concentration, but there are others that require a willingness to shift gears rapidly and think about more than one thing at once. Corporations, institutions, even nations are sometimes led successfully for a time by individuals who focus on single goals, but this narrowness is destructive in the long term. (Bateson 1989, 179)

Today's students face a complex future, and they will need to know how to do numerous things simultaneously. In addition, many of today's jobs and careers are transitory, and people will have to move on and adapt to new situations. They will need experiences, knowledge, and skills that will make them adaptable. Bateson notes, "Many of society's casualties are men and women who assumed they had chosen a path in life and found that it disappeared into the underbrush" (7).

Bateson's ideas provide us with an intriguing new model for the classroom—one that would integrate many interests and skills, balance many tasks, view all parts of our lives as important and worth developing, and promote the idea of integrating the components of our lives. The classroom would function as a three-dimensional setting for combining tasks rather than the old one-dimensional model that provides for one narrow career for life. Multiplicity is the stuff of modern life.

If Bateson is right, there is no better three-dimensional educational model than project teaching. A good classroom project is multiplicity personified, involving many facets of learning and of life itself, and producing a high level of satisfaction in achievement. What better place for students to begin composing their individual lives?

Gardner's Seven Intelligences

Howard Gardner, a Harvard psychologist, theorizes that the human brain possesses at least seven different kinds of intelligence, each of which governs a particular set of abilities, and each of which operates parallel to the others. Because each intelligence develops independently, a person may be high in one or more intelligences and low in others. Gardner's Seven Intelligences are:

1. Linguistic—an aptitude for using language.
2. Musical—an aptitude for enjoying, performing, or composing music.
3. Logical-mathematical—an aptitude for manipulating objects, relationships, patterns, categories, and symbols.
4. Spatial—an aptitude for perceiving and mentally manipulating objects, forms, or space in three-dimensional relationships.
5. Bodily-kinesthetic—an aptitude for using motor skills.

6. Interpersonal—an aptitude for understanding other people and getting along with them.

7. Intra-personal—an aptitude for understanding one's own feelings, thoughts, and ideas. (Gardner 1985, 73-76)

Gardner calls the concept of separate intelligences "modularity of mind," and he sees each module as "operating according to its own rules and exhibiting its own processes" (282). Furthermore, Gardner accepts D. Alan Allport's notion that each module is *content-dependent*; each kind of cognitive activity (intelligence) acts on specific kinds of information (281). This is in contrast to an older notion that broad skills such as "problem-solving" can be learned and applied to all kinds of abilities.

In a related idea, Gardner believes that originality or novelty nearly always occur within a single intelligence. Only occasionally does there appear to be someone who is an exception to this rule.

According to my own analysis, genuinely original or novel activities can come about only when an individual has achieved mastery in the field where he has been working. Only such an individual possesses the necessary skill and sufficient understanding of structure of the field to be able to sense where a genuine innovation will lie and how best to achieve it. (289)

A growing number of educators today accept Howard Gardner's concept of multiple intelligences. If in fact children do have multiple intelligences, then schools should design curricula that expose and exercise each of the intelligences. The project teaching described in this book can serve as the centerpiece for that kind of curriculum. In his book *The Unschooled Mind,* Gardner writes of the importance of projects in the school curriculum:

A number of themes characterize . . . projects . . . and should pervade an education for understanding from start to finish. Among these overarching themes are the recognition that children have different intellectual strengths and learn in different ways; that teachers must serve as role models of the most important skills and attitudes and must in a sense embody the practices that are sought; and that meaningful projects taking place over time and involving various forms of individual and group activity are the most promising vehicles for learning. (204)

Studies of the Brain and How Learning Takes Place

The study of the human brain and its functioning may indeed be the next frontier in educational research. Interest in brain research reached a high level when President Bush and the Congress designated the 1990s as the "Decade of the Brain." Early research on the brain was based upon cadavers, and later research explored the brains of live people who were undergoing brain surgery. One limitation on such research is that these brains have undergone physical damage or are otherwise abnormal. Up-to-date technology now permits researchers to look through the skulls of normal, living people and observe the live brain at work. New discoveries are now made almost daily, and anything written about the brain as long ago as three years is likely to be out of date. This research will continue for years to come, but a few solid findings have already emerged.

One important discovery is that the brain has considerable plasticity. During the 1970s, a Harvard professor speculated to his students that our brains are physiologically changed each morning, because we have assimilated the experiences of the previous day. This idea is no longer mere speculation. Research has verified that brain structure can change when the environment changes.

The findings of brain research make it clear that we should provide our students with enriched environments. An enriched environment provides added stimulation, which causes the brain to become more active and to develop in more complex and efficient ways. Students who engage in active (as opposed to passive) experiences learn more, understand more, and remember it longer.

The link to project teaching is obvious. The brain is a complex organ capable of and functioning most effectively when working on complex, real-life tasks. Besides being able to memorize (which some people equate with learning), the brain is able to distinguish patterns, analyze information, make judgements, create, and learn from experience. These are the outcomes of the enriched environment provided by project teaching. Ordinary "textbook" teaching most often requires only memorization, and provides few if any opportunities for the essential brain tasks described above.

The implications of brain research for education are too powerful to be ignored. The experiences that we provide for our students alter their brains in significant ways. What a stunning responsibility for those of us who sometimes reply, "Oh, I'm just a teacher." Just a teacher, indeed! We should reply to that too familiar "What do you do?" with a more specific reply. "I nurture minds." "I help develop children's brains." "I am currently working on a project to expand the minds of twenty-five children." And so on.

Redundancy of learning Redundancy is not always negative or unnecessary. In information theory, redundancy means presenting a message in several different ways in order to increase the possibility that it will be understood. In learning theory, *redundancy of learning* means giving the student (his or her brain, actually) several different ways to process information in order to increase the possibility that it will be learned.

We know that different children learn in different ways, and that not all children learn equally well in the same way. Redundancy of learning requires that we use a variety of approaches and examples when teaching a lesson, in order to increase the likelihood that an individual student will understand and learn. Then the lesson should be followed by choices of activities to extend or reinforce the learning.

Let us review some of the ways in which students acquire and process information. Any individual student may rely mainly on:

1. Reading and reflecting.
2. Reading and discussing.
3. Reading and writing.
4. Reading, writing, and sketching or drawing.
5. Looking at non-print materials and reflecting.
6. Looking at non-print materials and discussing.
7. Looking at non-print materials and imitating by sketching or drawing.
8. Listening and reflecting.

9. Listening and repeating.
10. Listening and discussing.
11. Listening, writing, and sketching or drawing.
12. Social interaction.
13. Problem solving.
14. Exploring and experimenting.
15. Creating.

This list is not exhaustive, but it illustrates the nature of the challenge that we face as teachers. Redundancy of learning requires that we provide a broad array of activities in order to meet the learning needs of all our students.

Learning and Memory

Learning relies upon memory, for without memory, learning cannot take place. One of the most vexing complaints by teachers is that students "don't remember anything that they studied last year." Or maybe yesterday. Too often, students learn something only long enough to take a test and then forget it. Research tells us that this need not be the case.

There are several kinds of memory: long-term and short-term, verbal and spatial, episodic and semantic, procedural and declarative, and a variety of other subdivisions. No matter what kind of memory we are concerned with, "the memory process is generally divided into three stages: coding, storage (or consolidation), and retrieval" (Hooper and Teresi 1986, 203–204). Educators tend to focus only on short-term and long-term memory, ignoring the others—and this is a mistake.

Short-term memory is only the beginning point of learning. It may last only a few minutes, or a few hours, but no longer than a couple of days. Furthermore, short-term memory seems to be limited to six or seven thoughts—"chunks of information." When more chunks are added before consolidation (converting the information to longer-term memory) some of the earlier thoughts are lost forever (Hooper and Teresi 1986, 203). Thus it is that most people remember very little after a lecture. The first part of the lecture is displaced in short-term memory by information that comes later, and, overall, only a few items are remembered.

When a student first "learns" something—anything—it goes into short-term memory. It is our challenge as teachers to help students consolidate this information—moving it into long-term memory, understanding, and true learning. To accomplish this change, the synapses must be stimulated repeatedly to produce a physical change in the synapses.

The hypothesis is that temporary electrochemical changes at the synapse can in time evolve into long-lasting *anatomical* changes. If a neuronal pathway is traversed over and over again, like a well-worn footpath, an enduring pattern is engraved. Neural messages tend to flow along familiar roads, along paths of least resistance. (Hooper and Teresi 1986, 196)

Shhhhh—rehearsal in session: building long-term memory

So, building long-term memory—and true learning—requires the neural pathways to be "traversed over and over again." Does this mean repetition? It certainly does. And repetition, which sounds a lot like drill and practice, is a favorite whipping boy in many educational circles today.

However, no matter what the critics say, information must be *rehearsed* in order to store it in long-term memory. There are several ways to rehearse information. One of the most common, and hated by generations of students, is recitation—repeating something over and over by rote until it sticks in the memory. It does work, of course. When I was an undergraduate, this was called "overlearning," and it was considered to be a useful technique when something needed to be memorized.

Today, elementary schools seem to be awash with worksheets, which provide another way to rehearse information. However, students tend to hate worksheets, and so do most professors of education. Actually there are good reasons to hate worksheets, including the mass murder of trees perpetuated to make them. Most worksheets require only passive mental activity. By contrast, students who *write* assignments "from scratch" (to abuse a phrase) are more mentally active, engage in more rehearsal, and consequently learn more than students who fill up worksheets.

Another major problem with recitation and worksheets is motivation. It is hard to motivate students to *want* to learn that way, and we can't make students learn when they don't want to. So how do we motivate students to rehearse information until it becomes a "familiar road," something remembered for the long haul, a part of "permanent" learning? Project teaching, of course.

Project teaching provides for many kinds of rehearsal. A student who is working on a project rehearses, consciously and unconsciously, mountains of information from many areas of the curriculum. Let us see how this might be done.

The student reads something of interest and takes notes. This is *rehearsal*. Discusses an idea with classmates. *Rehearsal*. Works on plans for building a model. *Rehearsal*. Discusses project with family. *Rehearsal*. Works on project. *Rehearsal*. Writes a report. *Rehearsal*. Prepares for Tour Day. *Rehearsal*. You get the idea.

And very rarely will a student ask, "Why do we have to learn this stuff?" Questions of meaningfulness and relevance have become irrelevant.

The Mind: Diamond in the Rough, or Polished Gem?

The diamond makes an interesting metaphor for the developing mind. When a diamond comes from the ground, its surface is rough and its shape irregular. The diamond must be cut and polished by a skillful craftsman to bring out its beauty. It is the facets (small sides) of the diamond that enable it to sparkle brilliantly, each facet cut and polished, each just the right size, shape, and angle. Most diamonds today have fifty-eight facets cut into their surface. This requires a lot of planning, skill, time, and patience by the diamond cutter.

And what of our students? Don't we find rough, irregular kids and try to increase their brilliance? By chipping a little here, polishing a little there, new facets emerge. The more facets, the more interesting the person, and as we like to think, the more brilliant. The diverse activities involved in project teaching—reading, writing, measuring, reflecting, problem solving, drawing, constructing—involve multifaceted thinking and learning. Those thoughts and activities etch themselves into the brain, creating a multitude of metaphorical facets.

Just suppose that students understood the metaphor of the brain as a diamond to be cut and polished. Can we persuade them to take charge of their own facets? When they delve into something new, they should think of it as developing a new facet of the mind. Rather than "learning" something for the teacher, the student should see the learning experience as personal development. The more facets students develop, the more interesting they become, and the more empowered.

The Project Method of Teaching and Learning

The project method of teaching and learning is a highly social enterprise. While reading about the processes and results, you may think of Lev Vygotsky and his ideas about the importance of social interaction for learning, and of the student's ability to learn by imitation, particularly when working as part of an active community of learners. Albert Bandura also included modeling (a kind of imitation) in his social learning theory.

A key feature of the project method is cooperative learning, not artificial and formularized, but based on social interaction and need. Children work together because they want to and have a purpose, not because they are assigned to do so.

As children work on a class project, individual differences become apparent in a variety of ways, lending weight to Howard Gardner's concept of multiple intelligences. Moreover, the project provides opportunities for each kind of intelligence represented in the classroom. Each student can work in his or her areas of strength and have those strengths valued by other class members.

Jean Piaget's ideas of cognitive development are recognizable as students actively explore and interact. Piaget believed that children gradually derive concepts and useful patterns of action through exploration of their environment. By solving problems encountered in the environment, children build cognitive structures and understanding.

Vygotsky noted also that human beings extend the capacity for memory past their biological structures by creating "signs," artificial objects that serve as reminders—a string around a finger, or a mark on a stick. Such simple memory aids can assist learning by extending the range of thought. More complex signs are used for remembering more complicated learnings. The classroom project is indeed a conglomerate of complex signs that reinforce memory and stimulate complex learnings.

In an extension of this idea, Vygotsky noted that "the very essence of civilization consists of purposely building monuments so as not to forget" (Vygotsky 1978, 51). In a real sense, the Washington, DC, project is a study of monuments that were built so that Americans would not forget important elements of their culture. What could be more appropriate in an active classroom than creating signs (via a project) to remember and study existing monuments of civilization?

Gestalt is an overarching feature of project teaching and learning, for both teacher and students. *Gestalt* is defined as a unified pattern having properties that cannot be derived from its parts. While working on a project, the student manipulates the mental and physical elements of the learning environment, making cognitive connections that lead to a gestalt—an insight into the connections and wholes of the project.

The teacher also must achieve a gestalt regarding a project, but on a different and more complex level, because of the responsibility of orchestrating the entire project. The first attempt at orchestration represents a journey into the unknown. There may be more activity than clarity, quite a lot of confusion, and moments of self-doubt. However, a gestalt develops gradually from the experience, and each subsequent project takes on additional meaning and refinement. Over time, the teacher will acquire a comprehension of the patterns, connections, and wholeness of the enterprise.

There is also the need for gestalt for the reader of *Constructing Buildings, Bridges, and Minds.* I confess that the book is not organized neatly into numbered steps, for that is not the way a project works, and it is not the way I teach. However, I hope the reader will achieve at least a modest "Aha!" while sharing my experiences with project teaching, and will be ready for the challenge.

1

Connections: Integrating the Subject Matter

This is the house that Pat built.

This is the work
That created the house that Pat built.

This is the scheme
That guided the work
That created the house that Pat built.

This is the theme
That governed the scheme
That guided the work
That created the house that Pat built.

These are the subjects
That embraced the theme
That governed the scheme
That guided the work
That created the house that Pat built.

These are the words, some short and some tall,
That marked the subjects
That embraced the theme
That governed the scheme
That guided the work
That created the house that Pat built.

These are the numbers, some large and some small,
That went with the words, some short and some tall,
That marked the subjects
That embraced the theme
That governed the scheme
That guided the work
That created the house that Pat built.

This is the map displaying the mall,
That was measured with numbers, some large and some small,

That went with the words, some short and some tall,
That marked the subjects
That embraced the theme
That governed the scheme
That guided the work
That created the house that Pat built.

This is the spot that started it all,
That was marked on the map displaying the mall,
That was measured with numbers, some large and some small,
That went with the words, some short and some tall,
That marked the subjects
That embraced the theme
That governed the scheme
That guided the work
That created the house that Pat built.

This is the building, remarkably tall,
That stood on the spot that started it all,
That was marked on the map displaying the mall,
That was measured with numbers, some large and some small,
That went with the words, some short and some tall,
That marked the subjects
That embraced the theme
That governed the scheme
That guided the work
That created the house that Pat built.

These are the famous, some known by all,
That worked in the building, remarkably tall,
That stood on the spot that started it all,
That was marked on the map displaying the mall,
That was measured with numbers, some large and some small,
That went with the words, some short and some tall,
That marked the subjects
That embraced the theme
That governed the scheme
That guided the work
That created the house that Pat built.

This is the art that hangs in the hall,
That ennobled the famous, some known by all,
That worked in the building, remarkably tall,

That stood on the spot that started it all,
That was marked on the map displaying the mall,
That was measured with numbers, some large and some small,
That went with the words, some short and some tall,
That marked the subjects
That embraced the theme
That governed the scheme
That guided the work
That created the house that Pat built.

— Virgil M. Young, with apologies to Mother Goose

*T*his rhyme cleverly demonstrates that all things are connected to something else. An integrated curriculum also demonstrates those connections, which may occur at many different levels. In its broadest sense, an integrated curriculum brings together the content and skills from the variety of subjects studied in a classroom.

Two major classroom projects are described in this book: one centering on Washington, DC, and the other encompassing all of Latin America. Each of these projects was a vehicle by which students integrated themselves into the world of making connections and enjoying learning. These two projects are presented to the reader as models, not prescriptions.

The Washington, DC, project was organized around the nation's capital and its symbols. This contrasts with the Latin America project, which was organized around the six strands of social studies: history; geography; government (political science); economics; sociology; and anthropology. The Washington, DC, project also contained elements of the six strands of social studies, but these were not the organizing principle. Readers are encouraged to develop their own unique projects suited to specific groups of students.

Connecting the Beginning with the End—
The Project Culmination

Before we get into a detailed explanation of the projects described in this book, let us first glimpse the most exciting part of a class project—the culmination. The culmination is the highlight of the project, an important event carefully planned to bring together—to connect—all of the learning accomplished by the students over an extended period of time. It should include activities that excite students, and it should provide them a chance to show off what they have learned. This implies an audience. Just as bands, orchestras, and choirs need public performances, and athletic teams need games and spectators to keep them motivated, academic motivation is heightened when students share their learning with caring adults.

So, welcome to Tour Day! The Tour Day you are about to visit is the culminating event of an extensive fifth-grade social studies project centered on Washington, DC, and it can serve as a model for a variety of other classroom projects.

Imagine yourself entering a unique classroom—the desks are missing, and in their place is a miniature city that students have designed and built. There are people everywhere amid the city—children and adults—talking, standing, kneeling, sitting on the floor. Listen to the energy in their voices, and look at the energy on their faces!

More people drift through the door—grandmas, babies, moms, dads, grandpas, aunts, uncles, neighbors, the mayor, anyone who has heard about this big event. The room vibrates with excitement. You can hear bits and pieces of conversation anywhere you stand in the room.

A man with a camera hesitates at the door, then smiles as his daughter rushes over to greet him. She grabs his hand and pulls him through the crowd. While he pauses to take pictures, she bursts forth with enthusiastic descriptions and explanations. At a building that looks remarkably like the White House, they bump into a mother and her son who are on their hands and knees peering inside. The roof has been removed, and a moment later all four people are on their knees looking at its furnishings.

"Look, the roof comes off the Supreme Court and there are the nine justices, and the woman is Sandra Day O'Connor, the first woman ever on the Supreme Court."

"Oops, excuse us. I want to take a picture of the Capitol with Jon sitting beside it."

"I measured the parts and glued them together. I studied a picture in a book to figure out how the Library of Congress looks. We even called the Library of Congress to ask some questions. The first books in the Library of Congress belonged to Thomas Jefferson because. . . ."

"Look, these are cherry trees along the Potomac River. All this blue plastic is the Potomac. Anyway, the trees were given to us by the Japanese."

"See this, Mom? I'm standing in front of the White House. Someone took our pictures, and we cut them out and glued them on sticks so it looks like we're standing in front of our buildings. See, there's Brandi standing by the Smithsonian."

The classroom is filled with people of all ages. Today it has become a true community of people with common interests, people who care about children and about learning. The students are excited because they have learned a lot (while they had a good time doing it), and now they have a chance to share their knowledge with adults who are interested. Today's event culminates almost a year of study. The adults are excited for the children and about what the children have learned. Many express astonishment at the depth and breadth of the children's knowledge, and they are impressed with the way the children express their learning. Not all the grown-ups are family members. Some are mindwise people who want to see and hear what the children learned.

Beware of eyewash   Classroom programs shared with parents are seductive, for they excite children and please parents. Unfortunately, not all such programs are culminations, and most parents don't know the difference. A program can easily be eyewash, a showy and happy event, but just an empty shell that does not connect prior learnings or culminate anything. It may make parents happy, but it is a waste of valuable time for both the teacher and the students. Worst of all, such empty eyewash programs demean learning and give project teaching a bad name. Unfortunately, many excellent teachers consider project teaching to be "fluff" because of the eyewash they have seen passed off as project teaching.

As you study the projects described here, you will see that there is no eyewash. Each detail of the culmination was preceded by the students' solid, worthwhile learning. A rule of thumb for the culmination—and for the entire project—is that if something does not have a valid educational purpose, if it makes no worthwhile connection, it should be omitted. However, there are plenty of wonderful things with valid educational purposes, and you will find no shortage of connections on the following pages.

Defining integration *Integration* refers to combining two or more disciplines into a single curriculum. Social studies is ideal for integrating a curriculum because not only do its six strands interact naturally and easily, but it can serve as a focus for nearly every other subject taught in the elementary/middle school. The integrated curricula described in this book encompass the following:

1. The subject matter, skills, and attitudes to be learned.
2. The philosophy and planning needed to teach the subject matter, skills, and attitudes.
3. The activities the students engage in to learn the subject matter, skills, and attitudes.

The Social Studies Connection

This entire book centers on social studies, which is a natural center of integration because it is the story of people and ideas, and the interaction and drama of their stories. Social studies is divided into six strands: history, geography, government, economics, sociology, and anthropology. I first began teaching about Washington, DC, with the modest intention of focusing on some history and government. But the project soon took on a life of its own, expanding into wider and wider areas and whole fields of knowledge, sweeping my students and me into a myriad of human experiences and stories until it was apparent that we should not be compartmentalizing this or that, but should be bringing everything together into the whole essence of life. What an opportunity to engage students in the celebration of life and ideas!

Project teaching, by using social studies as the center of a web of learning, is a highly effective way to connect and integrate the areas of reading, writing, literature, science, math, art, music, researching, oral communication, or anything else in your busy day. This rich mixture also creates opportunities for students to learn a variety of manipulative skills such as measuring, sketching, and cutting, and for a lot of incidental learning—interesting tangents from the main body of knowledge.

Is this a new idea? Scarcely. The Roman Marcus Aurelius wrote in A.D. 180, "All things are implicated with one another, and the bond is holy; and there is hardly any thing [sic] unconnected with any other thing."

Construction: A metaphor for building social studies

The research and construction of each building of the Washington, DC, project, and the many features of the Latin America project, provide a structure for the study of social studies. By doing research, each student becomes an expert on that particular portion of the project—its importance, use, content, people, and ideas. For instance, the National Museum of American History contains a trove of social studies treasures, and every other building or physical feature represents a story to be told.

Earlier in the fifth-grade year, before the project, we had studied the Revolutionary War and how our government was established and organized. Thus the students already knew about the Bill of Rights, the Constitution, and the three branches of government. They had a good grounding in the development of our country from the time of the Vikings until 1800. The knowledge and appreciations already gained helped launch us into the Washington, DC, project.

The history of the United States after 1800 was carried forward in the project through the students' work and discussions, as well as through explanations and stories that I provided. Washington, DC, served as the focus for learning about American history and government from the arrival of Columbus until the present. If you are wondering how Washington, DC, is related to Columbus, look at the eight panels on the bronze doors of the Capitol Building, which show the story of Columbus. Remember too that DC stands for District of Columbia, which was named after Columbus. In addition, the Capitol Building also contains artwork depicting the Revolutionary War and other events that predated the founding of Washington, DC.

As the project progressed, I gave students new information, adding to the old and pulling it all together. I told stories that connected with things we would study later. For instance, I told stories about Abraham Lincoln, and talked about the Lincoln Memorial, its columns, its inscriptions, the Civil War, and other highlights. The White House, Ford's Theater, the Petersen House, and the Lincoln Memorial are all tied to Lincoln, and Lincoln is tied to the Civil War. Later, when I taught about the Civil War, the Civil War had special meaning for them.

In this manner, I extended information and meaning for each of the buildings in the project through discussion, conversation, and storytelling. Mine was not a direct, linear presentation. Rather, I would weave information throughout, add to it, repeat it, and build on it, talking about Lincoln one day and Jefferson the next. However, rather than a lecture, it was a conversation between teacher and students. Students excitedly volunteered additional information that they had found in their reading and research. During these conversations, I helped them make connections and relationships. The students didn't become confused as to sequence, because we had a large time line across the front wall, and we always referred to it when discussing a person or event. Each of us felt a sense of joy in sharing our knowledge and contributing to the project.

Case studies in
social studies American history is rich with people whose lives are fascinating and instructive to study. Their biographies became our case studies. We read and discussed the difficult and tragic life of Abraham Lincoln; the life and times and achievements of George Washington; and the productive, varied, and inventive life of Thomas Jefferson. Other inspiring

stories included Paul Revere, Benjamin Franklin, Harriet Tubman, Clara Barton, Robert E. Lee, Lewis and Clark, Theodore Roosevelt, and Amelia Earhart, to name a few. The students loved to talk about their new friends encountered through such stories, friends who were real flesh-and-blood people much like ourselves, but who lived at an earlier time.

The Science Connection

The Smithsonian holds a wealth of ideas for incorporating science into the Washington, DC, project. We visited the Smithsonian museums from our own classroom via books, brochures, videos, and magazines, and the students chose wonderful science adventures and topics to explore. Let us look at the possibilities.

The National Air and Space Museum features rocketry, space, and flight. The National Museum of Natural History displays an infinite variety of natural phenomena, including mammals, sea life, birds, fossils, and an insect zoo, not to mention minerals, gems, meteorites, and a "Geologist's View of the Earth" on a huge relief globe. The National Museum of American History exhibits electricity, tools, and a large number of historic machines—steam engines, farm machinery, clocks, an undersea bubble chamber, an atom smasher, and a famous model of the Foucault Pendulum, to name just a few. In class, we discussed the museums and took a mental stroll through the Smithsonian and its wonderful avenues for science.

The National Zoo (the Smithsonian's National Zoological Park) was always of interest. The class would be intrigued with the animals, so we would end up having a unit on the zoo animals, their original habitats, and characteristics. Each year someone built the National Zoo, complete with animals, as part of the class project.

After surveying the Smithsonian, each student chose an individual science project and voted on a class science project. Each year's class seemed to have different interests. This did not matter, however, for each one had intriguing ideas for their science curriculum. And this is probably why it worked so well—their science was their own decision from this vast array of options. They made choices that *they* deemed important and that made connections to their world.

One year the students chose to work together on electricity. Another year it was fossils, and yet another, space flight. Thus through individual and class work, the students developed a personalized science curriculum characterized by personal investigation and collaboration. As tour guides at the end of the Washington, DC, project, they were full of science information and ideas when they came to the replica of the Smithsonian.

Case studies
in science   Biographies of scientists make excellent case studies that hook students on science. It is exciting to explore the world of telescopes and the universe with Maria Mitchell, lightning with Benjamin Franklin, electricity and light bulbs with Thomas Edison, and the telephone with Alexander Graham Bell.

Thomas Jefferson is an excellent case study to integrate science and social studies. Jefferson's life was the epitome of an integrated curriculum. Here we have a famous American who was a statesman, scientist, farmer, inventor, architect, musician, linguist, philosopher, writer, and promoter of the arts—and an innovative thinker who helped design our government. I read a biography of Jefferson to the class and also had books and articles available for the students to read. Jefferson's life demonstrates that the more you know, the more you can do. What a role model for kids!

The Math Connection

Teaching math should not be reduced to just doing problems in math class, but should help students understand the world around them. That is exactly what project teaching can do. So, what kind of math did we learn and apply in our projects? It included measuring, figuring scale, making maps, estimating, figuring perimeter and area, applying geometry, solving practical problems, making graphs, and calculating—adding, subtracting, dividing, and multiplying—whole numbers and numbers not so whole.

It should be understood that math skills weren't formally *taught* during social studies; after all, integration has its limits. Rather, we *used* math skills during the construction of the project. Math skills were learned in math class, then applied to the project.

Measuring and estimation

All kinds of math questions had to be asked in order to construct a building. How long? How high? How tall? What is length, width, and breadth? How many boxes of sugar cubes do I need? How much fabric do I need for the interior design? Such questions lead to figuring perimeters and areas.

Sometimes during math class I had the students draw floor plans of some of the buildings and figure the actual area and perimeter. From that, we estimated areas of cupolas and obelisks. The excitement of the project motivated the students to work on their math, and they readily transferred those math skills to their project. Skills transfer much more readily when students feel the need to apply them to something personal.

Scale and map making

The use of scale was of vital importance in building the city. The map of Washington, DC, (really the floor plan) had to be carefully drawn to scale. Each building had to be built within reasonable limits of size, though it was impossible to expect each building to be drawn exactly to scale. Chapter 2 suggests a rough scale for the buildings.

Large sheets of white butcher paper were laid on the floor for mapping the city. Students interested in laying out the city pored over maps of Washington, deciding how to measure and draw the tangle of streets, avenues, circles, and rivers. This required them to find directions, calculate measurements, use ratios, construct parallel lines, estimate, and problem solve. After drawing the overall map, the students located and marked the buildings that would become part of the project.

Geometry

In some years, we studied our geometry unit in math class prior to the project, while in other years, the geometry unit came later while we were working on the project. Both ways worked fine, since the students were able to transfer their geometry skills to the project.

Patterns for buildings had to be measured and cut. The students figured out how to cut triangles, rectangles, circles, and squares for making walls, roofs, windows, and adornments. For instance, the East Building of the Smithsonian is mainly designed from triangles, and the Hirshhorn building is a special challenge because it is shaped like a cylinder. Other challenges, such as how to make an obelisk or cupola, led to designing domes and shafts. Students became aware of the importance of space, since they all wanted their buildings to fit in the right spot.

Making graphs   As work on the project progressed, our classroom became a tourist stop for other students, teachers, parents, and a variety of other people who "just happened to be passing by." One year during math class, while we were studying graphing, Melinda suddenly exclaimed, "Why don't we graph our visitors?" The idea caught on, and the students began faithfully recording the number of visitors each day. Then they made graphs to show each week's visitors. Soon someone suggested that we categorize our visitors and make another graph showing the different categories. Thus we soon had a graph showing the number of students, teachers, brothers and sisters, friends, parents, and other adults. Quite a collection, and quite a graph!

This was only one of many possible ways to connect graphing to the project. A number of other details could have been counted and graphed, but our visitors kept us busy and interested.

Math awareness   Math is everywhere. Wherever we look or whatever we see, there is an angle or space or pattern or dimension. Students need to understand these relationships of math to their everyday world and to learn to recognize a mathematical event when they encounter one. In short, they need to develop the math awareness and habits of thinking that accompany them when they exit the classroom door.

The Art Connection

To **look** is one thing,
to **see** what you **look** at is another,
to **understand** what you **see** is a third,

to **learn** from what you **understand** is still something else;
to **act** on what you **learn** is all that matters.

(Taoist saying, Mittler 1989, 9)

Art is central to thinking. Too often, we have relegated art to a meaningless Friday afternoon activity. Creative art experiences help students develop observational skills and perceptions of the real world, including spatial relationships and three-dimensional thought. In order to plan, draw, construct, and paint their buildings, the students had to do a lot of looking, seeing, understanding, and learning. Their study of physical detail required 3-D thinking; they had to think about height, length, breadth, and other detail both literally and metaphorically. Since students write to learn, why shouldn't they likewise observe to learn?

When an actual skyscraper rises above a city, many specialties are involved. An architect creates a design; engineers work out exact measurements and materials and other details; workers of many kinds do the actual construction. In our project, the students did it all. And the art?

The buildings constructed by the students were artistic interpretations, not exact replicas. To fifth graders, this meant a model made from cardboard or sugar cubes or styrofoam or anything else that would work. We started with buildings seen only in photographs or drawings. Each student then developed a simplified plan that would catch the essence of the particular building, within the limits of his or her particular abilities and the construction materials available. Using these plans and other information gained through reading and research, we launched our city.

Art appreciation   Much of the art in Washington, DC, has historic significance. A great many paintings and statues depict important people and events that the students encounter. Who doesn't remember the painting of the signing of the Declaration of Independence, or of General Washington crossing the Delaware? How do we know what Washington, Jefferson, and Franklin looked like? We know only from paintings and sculptures made during their lifetimes. Artists have left us wonderful records of history.

Washington, DC, has numerous art museums and galleries, which can provide excellent opportunities to expand the students' knowledge and appreciation for art. With this in mind, we took Washington, DC, gallery walks to discover, enjoy, and learn about famous art and famous artists. The Smithsonian is an ideal environment for seeing art as well as history and science. The Smithsonian boasts of several outstanding art museums, including the world famous National Gallery of Art, Freer Gallery of Art, and Hirshhorn Museum and Sculpture Garden. In addition, the Capitol has over 300 paintings on its walls.

How do you take a Smithsonian gallery walk in Boise, Idaho? We had many sources to draw from. I had found some picture books, art books, and calendars with art from the Smithsonian on sale tables here and there. (Calendars especially are a bargain in June.) Because the students had already developed an affinity for the Smithsonian through history and science, they were also interested in learning about the art.

Imagine fifth graders strolling along the walls of the classroom, gazing at paintings of Abraham Lincoln, Frederick Douglass, Henry David Thoreau, and Chief Joseph. "Who is Frederick Douglass?" "Who is Thorough [sic]?" "Hey, here's Chief Joseph!" (Chief Joseph was important in Idaho history.) Thus we have the beginnings of some very interesting conversations.

Imagine fifth graders encountering the works of Rembrandt, Picasso, Monet, and Renoir at the National Gallery of Art. Or visiting the Hirshhorn to see the work of Mary Cassatt and Georgia O'Keeffe. Or walking through the sculpture garden at the Hirshhorn. The experiences we simulated led to new worlds and remarkable class conversations.

After our gallery walks—and conversations—the books and pictures were left on a table for the students to study further. Some became tattered and fell apart, but we still used them. Later, as they were constructing buildings that contained artwork, many students sketched pieces of the work and placed them inside. As a result of seeing and working with art in a variety of ways, the students learned to value art as a connection to our world and to our lives.

The Music Connection

Music can add a sparkling dimension to a project, but the music must relate to the subject matter being studied. For ours, I located records and tapes of music from Revolutionary and Civil War times, as well as other music of Americana, both early and modern. Students especially loved to sing "This Land Is Your Land" and "Yankee Doodle," but enjoyed singing and listening to many others. While not all songs of Americana relate directly to Washington, DC, American folk songs and sagas add an important flavor to the study of America, which in our case was personified by Washington, DC.

Over the years, I introduced a variety of songs, some more successful than others. The favorites included: "The Star Spangled Banner," "Dixie," "Camptown Races," "Bluetail Fly," "Oh! Susanna," "The Battle Hymn of the Republic," "When Johnny Comes Marching Home," "Turkey in the Straw," "John Henry," "I've Been Working on the Railroad," "The Yellow Rose of Texas," and "We Shall Overcome."

The Reading Connection

Reading permeated the project. We read anything and everything we could find on Washington, DC—books, magazines, brochures, and newspapers. We became reading sleuths, snooping everywhere for just one more piece of intriguing information to add to our project. Our reading included all the areas of integration, and we read with many varied purposes in mind. Each student had a folder for reading material, and when one of us ran across something pertinent to someone else's area, I would make a photocopy for the appropriate research folder. This turned out to be a great motivator for students. They loved finding information about a classmate's project and sharing their finds.

I also encouraged the students to read historical fiction by reading them books that fit into their projects. For example, *Johnny Tremain, War Comes to Willy Freeman, My Brother Sam Is Dead, The Story of Abraham Lincoln*, and *The Root Cellar* are wonderful stories to get fifth graders interested and involved in social studies subject matter. Often times, these stories motivated students to write some historical fiction of their own.

The Writing Connection

If we want students to develop a true interest in what we are teaching, and an intelligent comprehension of what they are learning, they must write about it. So, along with the building, researching, and reading, we embraced writing.

Writing is the glue of integration. During our projects, writing blurred the divisions between language arts, social studies, and the other subjects. *In language arts, we learned to write. In social studies and science, we wrote to learn.* So which time was which? In the end, we just wrote and wrote without worrying about what classroom period it was or which subject we were "studying." This was integration at its finest.

Research and note taking

All students worked on some aspect of the project. For example, the student who had the Capitol Building would be learning and researching the legislative branch, the art in the Capitol, the Columbus or Bronze doors, the people who write our laws, the Senators and Representatives from Idaho, the Trumball art, Statuary Hall, the Statue of Freedom, the architecture, or anything else pertinent. (And some people think projects are Mickey Mouse!) The student who had the National Archives would be learning and researching the Declaration of Independence, the Constitution, and the Bill of Rights, and how this building is constructed to preserve these documents.

Research of this kind means a lot of note taking. However, before you envision note cards, let's talk about how the students took notes. Each student kept a research journal with his or her notes written in it. I gave the class a short lesson in organizing notes, stressing that they needed to arrange their notes into separate topics, use clearly marked headings, and leave plenty of space in the margins and between paragraphs. The spacing was important so they could go back and insert questions, comments, or additional details if needed.

Many students made pretty sketchy notes at first, but after they warmed up to their topics, they soon realized how important and useful the notes could be. After that, most research journals grew rapidly and blossomed like fields of wildflowers—filled with interesting, colorful, often untidy, and not always predictable specimens.

Sources of information   Where did students get all of the information for their research? Before beginning the project, I had assembled a variety of resource materials. Thus the students had ready access to books, magazines, and videos. The *National Geographic* was especially valuable, and we located about a truckload of back issues in a local thrift shop, which sold them for ten or fifteen cents a copy.

I also assembled packets of things I found (often scrounged) that would help in the research. These packets might contain pictures, articles, brochures, addresses, book titles, or anything else that seemed appropriate. The students also went to the school library for research. At other times, when students discovered an adult in the school or community who could provide useful information, they interviewed that adult and jotted notes into the research journal.

As the students gathered more and more information, they became more focused on what they wanted to know, and they began to ask questions and read with these questions in mind. They were usually researching two or three questions at any given time. They frequently inserted questions into their journals, hoping they might find that important piece of the puzzle.

Periodically I would collect the journals and write questions to nudge thinking, suggest new materials for researching, and comment on the interesting progress of the research. Each time we had community discussions, students came up with new questions to answer. Information that seemed valuable was recorded in their research journals, whether from resource materials or from classmates or from adults.

Sometimes I had a bulletin board where students posted notices of topics they were interested in, or things they had found that might interest someone else. Someone once pinned up a photocopy of the Capitol Building under construction with a note, "Guess when." More commonly the bulletin board contained notices by individuals announcing that they had found certain kinds of information:

"See Wendy for pictures of Washington, DC, at cherry blossom time."

"See me for information on the Treasury Building. Jason."

Occasionally notices were creative:

"Wanted Dead or Alive: John Wilkes Booth or information on his whereabouts."

"For Sale: Information on Ford's Theater. Meet me by the dumpster at recess. Bring money."

It was stimulating to see all these kids reading, writing, thinking, and sharing for a purpose. Through experience, they were learning that writing is a useful form of expression, and increasingly they found satisfaction and pleasure in that written expression.

Writing for integration

The students engaged in a wide variety of writing activities that helped develop their writing skills while they were integrating information from other areas of the curriculum. For example, the historical fiction that I read aloud often stimulated the students to write skits and plays about the stories and characters. Students wrote and produced play after play, for which they made costumes and props and wrote parts, dialogue, and stage directions. Some students wrote their own fictional stories based on real events and real people.

Year after year, my students wrote letters to our U.S. Senators and Congressmen, asking all kinds of questions and explaining their projects. The response was overwhelming. The staff of each Senator and Congressman took the students' letters very seriously. They gathered brochures, pictures, and pamphlets and mailed them to the students, and often sent personal letters.

From their experiences with letters, the students learned that clear, thoughtful writing gets more attention and is likely to be answered. And were the students excited when they received their answers! When anyone received a letter or material in the mail, we all gathered excitedly to hear about it. Everything that was received was shared—and sometimes the information was just the piece someone else had been looking for.

Another writing and integrating technique that I used was the *exit paragraph*. This is an effective writing technique, but it should not be used every day. Like any other technique, it loses effectiveness when used too often.

Sometimes, before students left the classroom for the day, I had them write an exit paragraph. Here are some examples:

1. Questions that baffle them.
2. A summary of what they have been working on this week.
3. Two answers that they have found.
4. Two solutions that they have found.
5. New questions they are asking.
6. How their research changed as they learned more.
7. A three- or four-line news story about their project.
8. A source they found that would help another classmate in research and note taking.
9. A description of a picture that helped them in their research.
10. A description of an interesting way they found a solution.
11. Research sources they have found outside of the classroom.

It is important to give the students enough time so they aren't just scribbling something in order to get out of the room. I liked to put the assignment on the board in the morning so they could ponder it and write about it during the day. Then they handed it to me as they left for the day. Before long, the students became accustomed to writing and thinking on paper.

Writing for Tour Day On Tour Day the students took visitors on tours of the entire Washington, DC, or Latin America project. The extensive and varied writing experiences throughout the year prepared the students well to serve as tour guides. To prepare for the actual tour, the students wrote rehearsals of things they especially wanted to say and jotted down ideas for giving something a certain twist. They certainly didn't write everything down, for a tour would often take an hour or two. Neither did they use their papers for the tour, since they knew the information by heart. In the years since, many former students have told me that they remember a great deal about Washington, DC, and several who later visited the actual city were amazed to find it a familiar and friendly place.

Connecting Different Points of View

Specialists in different fields of study—the historian, the scientist, the artist, and others—will each see the world differently. It is good for students to be exposed to such a range of points of view. Where does a classroom teacher find such people? Everywhere! After all, we do live in an educated society. I had no trouble finding wonderful guest speakers and valuable resource people. They came from the local university; they were people from business and industry; they were parents, hobbyists, retired people, and volunteers. Given an opportunity, people with special knowledge and skills are eager to come to school and share their expertise.

We had parents who traveled to Washington, DC, on business and came back loaded with books, pictures, pamphlets, postcards, anecdotes, and fresh ideas. We had an architect explain how to plan a building and a lawyer explain how to build a government. An artist showed us how to see things like an artist. A nurseryman explained about different kinds of cherry trees. Our U.S. Congressman came one day and presented our classroom with an American flag that had been flown over the U.S. Capitol.

On one occasion, a political science professor came to answer student questions about the beginnings of our government. He temporarily forgot who his audience was and asked the class how many had read *The Federalist* papers. The professor and I were both shocked to see one student raise his hand; the student actually had looked at a volume of *The Federalist.* After this experience, the professor expressed amazement at the excitement, curiosity, and knowledge of the students. He said that these fifth graders asked better questions than his university students did. What better evidence of the power of project teaching to inspire motivation and learning!

Don't be afraid to ask people to share their knowledge and skills with your class. Some friends have been amazed that I would call up people I didn't know and ask them to come and talk to my students. But it works. I have never been turned down, and the guests always gain something from the experience, too.

Final Connections

So many things connect to other things. In a broad sense, integration is living, working, and learning together, and my fifth-grade children learned to do just that. In fact, that may have been the most important lesson they learned. Isn't that what social studies is all about?

The project wasn't truly integrated until the students had a vision of the whole city. Each student had to know more than just his or her own small piece. In order for students to know about everyone's work, some important things had to happen. First, the students discussed among themselves what they were doing. They did this by moving around the room, talking to others, and asking questions. They were free to do this during work sessions. I assisted by adding interesting material through direct teaching at favorable moments, and stimulating the class conversations. These activities helped weave together diverse strands and build important connections.

A Novel Approach

You have now seen the possibilities of an integrated curriculum in action. Among the many plans for integrating curriculum, this is a novel approach—novel in more than one sense of the word. Not only is it novel in the sense of being unusual, but it also carries elements of a well-written novel—setting, characters, plot, action, and resolution. Through active learning, my students and I lived these elements.

The plan   A novel must be well planned, and there was a definite plan that led to the opening scene in this chapter. The plan was based on an overall conceptualization of active, participatory learning and the development of intrinsic motivation. The participatory learning was structured to help students learn large amounts of subject matter in both depth and breadth. At the same time, the activities encouraged reading, research skills, cooperation, critical thinking, and creativity.

The projects integrated as many fifth- or sixth-grade subjects as possible into an experience of *whole learning*. Whole learning, as I use it, means learning two or more subjects together without the artificial divisions found in much of our curriculum. The term is related to *holistic,* which stresses the interdependence of the parts that make up a whole. The structure used for integration was social studies; however, language arts, reading, science, math, art, music, research, and writing all became integral parts of the learning experience. Whole learning is a step beyond the usual suggestions for integrating curriculum.

The actual project work and construction began in January and culminated in May. However, we spent the entire school year thinking and learning and developing skills necessary for the project. We could not have begun the project in January without the knowledge we accumulated during the first semester. After the project work began, earlier learning began to crystallize, interrelationships took on reality, and real learning intensified. I say real learning, because numerous former students, years later, vividly recall many of the things learned in their fifth- or sixth-grade projects.

Participatory Learning

Participatory learning means *active* learning—students participating in their own education. The students *do* active things that result in learning. It also means that their activities are well plotted; students are not left entirely to their own devices. The metaphor of the novel illustrates some of the facets of active learning. The project contained the elements of suspense, intrigue, action, dialogue, and, yes, even a happy ending.

Suspense   My fifth- and sixth-grade "characters" worried about how their creations would turn out. Could they finish their buildings on time? Would the frosting mix hold the sugar cubes until Tour Day? Would they forget what to say when they were Tour Guides? What if the classroom mice escaped from their cage and ate the buildings? The tingle of suspense gave the enterprise an edge of excitement, and, remarkably, the results always turned out to be excellent.

Intrigue   Curious minds searched for the answers to many questions. "How do you. . . ?" "What if. . . ?" "Why did. . . ?" These were questions students asked each and every day. Intrigue is a necessary element in problem solving.

Dialogue   Dialogue is essential for communication of ideas. Never was there a problem with dialogue for thirty fifth or sixth graders. (We just called it talking.) My natural teacher fear was that students weren't talking about what they were supposed to be talking about. I became Sherlock Holmes, snooping and eavesdropping, but almost always found that the right story was in progress.

The dialogue we spoke was a language of ideas, plans, construction, building, measuring, dreaming, what if's, and maybe not's. It was whole learning, free from the contradictions of short time periods for each subject, quick affairs with information never to be seen or used again, and interrupted thinking. Just as New York City or Boise or Boston weren't alive until created from the ideas of their people, neither were the Washington, DC, and Latin America projects alive until created from the ideas of the students—each having a story to tell.

Action   There was plenty of action—constructive action. During the time devoted to working on their projects, it was a rare student who was idle or wasting time. The room literally buzzed with activity. To the surprised visitor who wandered into the classroom, it was a chaotic scene: students everywhere moving about, cutting, gluing, painting, carrying things, working alone, talking—a few reading or drawing or taking notes—everyone doing something.

Happy ending   Our happy ending was Tour Day. On Tour Day, the students celebrated their achievements—achievements in what they had learned, and achievements in what they had created. Each student became a teacher and expert tour guide for visitors. Dozens of people—almost anyone and everyone—were invited to tour Washington, DC, or Latin America.

Every child anxiously awaited a family member to come and share his or her joy, and only a few children were disappointed. For those children, I could always find a kind adult who would listen attentively and give praise where praise was due. Sometimes a tour would take up to two hours, because the tour guide insisted on explaining everything he or she knew about the project. The students experienced the rich feelings—intrinsic rewards—of having learned something that has meaning. Tied to these feelings was the joy of *knowing*—a liberating experience.

Beyond Making Excuses—Overcoming Inertia

Most of us suffer from natural inertia, even when we know we ought to make changes in the way we do things. It is easy to find excuses for not taking action. Below is a list of thoughts that can discourage taking on a major classroom project.

1. The children won't behave.
2. There isn't time.
3. The classroom isn't the right shape.
4. What will the principal say?
5. What if the students don't score well on achievement tests?
6. Somebody might criticize me.
7. I don't think I can carry off this kind of project.
8. What if my bulletin boards suffer?
9. I have too many students this year.
10. I can't live with a messy classroom.
11. What if paint gets on the floor?

You see that the list can become endless. Excuses get in the way of progress. We have a choice between falling into the old hand-wringing "woe is me" rut, or we can jump out of the rut and try experimenting with how kids learn. After many years of serpentining around stuff on the floor, I discovered some rather amazing things. Below are antidotes to the excuses listed above.

The children won't behave My students didn't always behave when I used traditional methods of teaching. I discovered that my classroom management problems were much fewer when all the students were involved and committed to this kind of learning. Everyone was too busy with interesting work to get involved in any important behavioral problems. Students were busy figuring out their tasks and sharing ideas with classmates.

There isn't time Time looms over every teacher. We are asked to do more and more, while nothing is removed from our tasks. If you want to teach more in less time, try the project method. For one thing all the interruptions—pictures, assemblies, announcements, money-making schemes, and whatever else someone somewhere (whose job appears to be thinking of ways to interrupt your day) dreams up—won't be so maddening. The students can easily pick up where they left off—without a lot of reorienting. I often wonder how much the Director of Interruptions gets paid—it must be a lot, since he or she is so highly skilled.

The classroom isn't the right shape

When one thinks of a classroom, a rectangle or square usually comes to mind. These common shapes are very adaptable to project-on-the-floor teaching. However, the room that gave me the most trouble was a sort of triangle-shaped room. It wasn't easy, but we made it work. If you can do project-on-the-floor teaching in a triangle, you can do it anywhere.

What will the principal say?

I have used project teaching with three different principals who had, shall we say, very different personalities. These might loosely be defined as "not give a rip," "tight ship," and "loose democratic." All three were absolutely supportive and couldn't have done more to help me. Even the "not give a rip" personality surpassed my highest hopes on Tour Day. A lot will be overlooked if kids are learning.

What if the students don't score well on achievement tests?

I assure you that we always covered the required curriculum, but I decided to erase test phobia from my mind. I knew that life would be a lot happier if I weren't worrying every day about my students knowing this or that answer. Instead, we started making connections in our learning. Often it was more effective to teach two or more subjects together than to teach them separately. Children began to see patterns in knowledge and to develop their own conceptual frameworks. Guess what. Their achievements test scores shot up.

Somebody might criticize me

If you can find someplace in this life where you won't be criticized, it won't be in teaching. Don't worry about being criticized; confound your critics. Discover the best system for you to teach and for your students to learn. Then proceed with all your skill and enthusiasm. It helps to remember some of those irritating truisms: "Criticism helps us grow." "If you don't take risks and make mistakes, you won't grow and learn." "It's easier to criticize than to be correct."

I don't think I can carry off this kind of project

You will find that the kids will carry it off for you. It isn't your project; it is theirs. They are extremely creative and clever if given the opportunity. So what if by chance it didn't meet your standards? You can't predict how skillful your students will be when using an exacto knife, gluing walls and windows, or painting details on buildings. What really matters is that the students are learning by doing. The amount of learning will vary from student to student, but that also happens when you teach by conventional methods.

What if my
bulletin boards
suffer?

This was never a concern of mine. A teacher has only so much energy. You must decide if your energy should go to stimulating children's minds, or into bulletin boards designed to get "oohs" and "aahs" from everyone in the district. A teacher friend once remarked of her school, "My God, you have to be an interior decorator to teach there."

Choose the epitaph you would rather have on your tombstone:

1. "Always beautiful bulletin boards."
2. "His/her students learned to think and live."

Besides, kids never pay much attention to your bulletin boards; they like their own. So forget being nominated Bulletin Board King or Queen.

I have too many
students this year

You'll be sorry if you use this as an excuse. Your students won't be learning as much with conventional methods anyway, and it will probably be a very dull and frustrating year.

Don't worry about size. Adapt to what you have. A classroom is like a goldfish bowl; whatever the size of the bowl, the fish grow to fill it up. Use unconventional space. You can hang things from the ceiling, use the walls, and run "clothesline" wires overhead across the room. Maybe you can use part of the hall. If all else fails, make the city smaller. I'm not suggesting that you build Boise instead of Washington, DC; just adapt a smaller scale for Washington, DC.

I can't live with a
messy classroom

Sure you can. It depends on your definition of messy. To me, messy means having stuff all over, but the "stuff" is making active learning possible. I would much rather have children learning actively than to have a showplace classroom where not much happens to young minds. After all, you can have the children do some cleaning and straightening at the end of each day.

What if paint gets on the floor? It will be a miracle if paint doesn't get on the floor. If it does? The person who spilled the paint simply cleans it up. My classroom carpet has a few faded spots, but these serve as warm memories of important things accomplished. A carpet spot seems like a small issue when we compare it with students bored to tears by worksheet upon worksheet.

2

Designing and Planning the Washington, DC, Project

My model [the Washington Monument] was built of sugar cubes and white frosting and stood nearly two and a half feet high. I developed more than one killer stomachache working with my sweet building materials, but it certainly was fun! The report was given orally, then turned in for the written part of the assignment. At the time, the unit seemed to be just plain fun. The trick was that we were learning all along. Looking back now as a student teacher, I see the unit in an entirely different light. I see the project as the epitome of integration across the curriculum. The unit involved oral and written communication skills, art (design and creativity), and U.S. history. From an educational perspective, it couldn't have been better.

— Tim Lowe, former student

*I*ntegrating different subject matter requires a lot of thought and planning by both teacher and students. I don't mean the ivory tower planning that you read about in some books and journals. I mean nuts-and-bolts planning: deciding on themes, locating materials and resources, thinking of productive student activities, and making a plan of attack. This is not ivory tower talk. This comes from a teacher who has spent time on her knees with a glue gun in her hand.

The actual construction of the project began in January, drawing on learnings begun in September. Construction—absorbing ideas, integrating knowledge, and expanding minds—continued until May. Culmination day (Tour Day) came in May, often after a last-minute rush to get the final details in place.

Making Curriculum Choices

Planning requires making curriculum choices. Though both teacher and students are involved in planning, it is the teacher who knows the scope of the required curriculum and the structure of the disciplines. Thus the teacher is responsible for leading the students to an understanding of the possibilities. I set broad limits for the subject matter, and the students made choices freely within those limits. Even at that, when a student made a well-reasoned request to work outside those limits, I was happy to accept it.

For the Washington, DC, project, I read my fifth-grade social studies text to figure out blocks of time and logical breaking points. I selected 1800 as the dividing point: the project began where the earlier phase of learning ended. Why 1800? Maybe 1821 or 1755 would have worked. Possibly, but 1800 was the year Thomas Jefferson was elected President, and I saw this as a turning point in history.

Following is a list of important items, occurring before and after 1800, that became parts of the project. (Many other items were taught also.)

Items before 1800	Items after 1800
Christopher Columbus	The War of 1812
The Mayflower Compact	The Civil War
Religious Freedom	Emancipation Proclamation
Slavery	Abraham Lincoln
French and Indian War	World War I
George Washington	World War II
Revolutionary War	Korean War
Thomas Jefferson	Vietnam War
The Declaration of Independence	
Benjamin Franklin	
Articles of Confederation	
Constitution of the United States	
The building of Washington, DC	

This was the Janus approach to teaching. From the year 1800, we looked back at a lot of material, and at the same time we also looked ahead to what was coming. A time line was an important tool for helping students see the relationships of time and events.

The students and I made a list of all the buildings, monuments, memorials, and whatever else we wanted to include. Then each item was written on a separate slip of paper and placed in a hat. At the appropriate time, each student drew one of the slips of paper out of the hat (or bag or whatever was handy), and that became his or her task for Washington, DC. Some students volunteered for more than one slip.

Why didn't I assign the students what I thought they could do, or why didn't I let them choose? Because drawing slips from a hat is entirely fair. The students knew there was no teacher favoritism in making the assignments. Even when students *are* allowed to "choose," the teacher is still placed in the position of showing favoritism when two or more students want the same task. Occasionally, my students would negotiate and trade project tasks—which was another worthwhile learning experience. Assignment by lottery preserved the self-esteem of every student and avoided student quarrels about who gets what.

Brainstorming and Researching

Brainstorming and researching were our next steps. Students need time to work out plans, think of many ways to do an assignment, try out some of their plans and ideas, and discard them all and try again if a better approach appears. Too often we ask students to make snap decisions, to stay with those decisions, and to get the work finished before recess. Learning, thinking, and innovation must be given time. Students need to see that their creative work can change over time.

The students need visual help—pictures of what they are going to design—and they need to do a lot of reading about their project. As the project presses forward, you'll find that the students are going to public libraries, and parents are getting involved in the search and the discussions. However, you, the teacher, must provide most of the resources. These include books, magazines, articles, pamphlets—any material available for the specific projects that the students are working on. I collected a huge amount of material on Washington, DC, and had it available in the classroom for use and reference. Often a student would take material home and pore over it for ideas. I kept a lot of the research material in plastic laundry baskets that could be plowed through by students and also whisked away into a cupboard or stashed somewhere if we needed to present an appearance of tidiness for a visitor who might look askance if we appeared messy and busy.

Finding research materials   Where do you find research materials? Everywhere! As a teacher you become a researcher along with the students. You visit book stores and seek out thrift shops that sell out-of-print materials. Back issues of *National Geographic* are treasure troves for this project, and our local thrift shops seemed to have an endless supply. You write to addresses in Washington, DC, and cut out articles from the newspaper, and soon everyone else is doing the same thing, and your laundry baskets begin to overflow with information on Washington, DC. These materials are used by the students.

Don't try to protect the materials, because then they won't be used. If something from a book is important, but you shudder at seeing the book under the glue gun or next to white paint, then make copies of the text—but allow students the pleasure of digging in and using information.

Using Mixed Teaching Strategies

At this point, the students know what their individual projects are, materials have been gathered, and there is a high degree of motivation. What comes next? Optimum learning comes from a rich mixture of teaching strategies.

In broad terms, we used a mixture of (1) direct instruction, (2) group activities, and (3) discovery learning. Each of these three broad terms encompasses a number of specific teaching/learning strategies.

Direct instruction   Direct instruction is necessary to build a reservoir of knowledge that the student can apply. The knowledge shared through direct teaching is to be used, not just memorized; it is knowledge developed into concepts that students can understand and work with.

As project work progressed, I taught selected lessons on history, government, people, geography, children's literature, and anything else that seemed pertinent to our study. Many of these lessons were direct teaching. Following are some examples:

1. Reading assignments
2. Writing assigned tasks
3. Taking notes
4. Exploring oral and/or written questions that build comprehension
5. Making generalizations
6. Participating in class discussions

Group activities   Much of the project work was cooperative and collaborative. Students helped one another in every phase of the work—planning, research, construction, practicing tour speeches—you name it. When research had begun in earnest, you would often hear people exchanging research material: "Where's Tony? Here's something about the Potomac River that he can use." During construction of the buildings, it was common for students to help each other back and forth—offering suggestions, working out scales or designs, helping with cutting or gluing, and any number of other problem-solving activities. Often they would walk around to admire other people's work.

Students interested in mapping and scaling went to work laying out the city on paper on the floor (applying math skills, of course). This cooperative effort became the foundation of the project, showing streets and other features that would guide the later placement of buildings. Almost everyone was interested in the map, and the students working on this aspect never ran out of advice from other class members. Later, as the buildings were completed, students worked together to get each building in just the right spot on the map.

Brainstorming was common. "What kind of material should I use to build. . . ?" "Where can we get cardboard boxes?" "Whose mom or dad can take us to the mall?" Conning parents was a frequent topic. It was fascinating to listen to—all without the teacher's interference.

They also liked to discuss things they were learning. More than once, I was ready to break up a group of talkers, only to overhear something like, "Washington did too burn down. The British soldiers did it!" Did somebody really say that children don't learn anything important from each other? Following are some of the group strategies that we used.

1. Whole-group orientation
2. Classroom maintenance chores
3. Small-group cooperative learning
4. Small-group collaborative construction
5. Classroom brainstorming

Discovery learning Each student had to research his or her building. Closed-ended inquiry included finding out the size and shape of the building, the materials it was made from, its history, and why it was important or interesting. Open-ended inquiry included discovering interesting information about a particular historical person, and perhaps trying to decide how important that person was.

Research often began with the encyclopedia, but it quickly spread to other books, newspapers, and magazines—especially the *National Geographic*. Students learned to analyze photographs and drawings, maps, and written descriptions. Most wrote to their Congressmen or U.S. Senators for information. One enterprising researcher called the Library of Congress in Washington, DC, and got information over the phone!

Problem solving often took a creative dimension. How do you make a model building look like it is made of brick? How do you make the interior of a building look authentic given the limitations of size, materials at hand, lack of clear-cut information, and limited artistic ability? Students tackled such problems head-on and came up with clever and innovative solutions. Additional creativity was required to write narratives and stories and to prepare presentations for Tour Day.

The development of civic values was another important outcome of the project. The values of good citizenship were not taught didactically, but were acquired gradually. On a day-to-day basis, students learned to work together, sometimes cooperatively, and often through the accommodation of one another's differences. On a larger scale, values began to accumulate as students studied and admired many of our important historical figures—heroes, if you like. As students studied the U.S. Constitution and the founding of our government, they marveled at the wisdom of our "founding fathers." They began personalizing our democratic system, taking pride in being a part of it, and expressing opinions about the rights and responsibilities of citizenship.

Below I have compiled a list of specific discovery activities, but when I look back on the last several paragraphs, it seems impossible to limit any of the descriptions to any one of the discovery activities. This illustrates the fact that several kinds of learning can occur together, especially during discovery—and especially when curriculum is truly integrated.

1. Reading to discover information
2. Writing to aid thinking
3. Learning research skills
4. Developing civic values
5. Closed-ended inquiry
6. Open-ended inquiry
7. Descriptive research
8. Historical research
9. Problem solving
10. Creative efforts
11. Independent study

Finding Work Space

With all the things spread out over the classroom floor, where did the students do their work? Where did we put their desks?

While the students were working on the project, the desks were crowded together around the edges of the classroom. My desk and the two work tables also were squeezed to the edge of the room. As the project grew, the amount of space for desks and tables shrank. It was a challenge for students to work at their desks, but nobody ever complained.

Just before Tour Day, all the student desks were taken out of the classroom and stored along a wall in the hallway. With the desks out of the room, the project could be spread out, adjusted, repaired, and prepared for presentation. On Tour Day, the students who were not giving tours often rested on the floor around the edges of the room to watch and listen to the tours in progress. Sometimes they would read or talk quietly among themselves. Almost every student, however, would check around and try to be helpful when needed.

Looking in on a Busy Classroom

Let us join a classroom full of eager architects and builders with glue guns, paint, and exacto knives ready to cut loose. At first glance, it may seem that no one is in charge of the room. If you think a classroom should be completely quiet and tidy, you may not want to stay, and you might even feel pity for someone who would try such an enterprise. Granted, this type of teaching is not for the faint hearted. On the other hand, if you find excitement in seeing children experience the joys of learning and of furnishing their minds, this is for you.

Obviously, the teacher must be in charge of the situation. However, students have a great deal of freedom to move about and talk. Guidelines are necessary for the project to succeed, and these have already been worked out with the students. After watching the class for several minutes, you will discern patterns to the activities.

The Construction Process

We have gathered all kinds of stuff for our workshop. The students have assembled a variety of construction materials gathered from everywhere—cardboard, PVC pipe, modeling clay, twigs, and anything else they think might come in handy. Most materials were free, scrounged from homes and from store dumpsters. Cardboard was a versatile and universal favorite, and so were scraps of paper, wood, and styrofoam. Students also found uses for drinking straws, crepe paper, plastic wrap, and the paper cylinders left from rolls of bathroom tissue and paper towels. Parents often invested in boxes of sugar cubes, cake frosting mix, and popsicle sticks. Later as students began work on interiors, materials such as wallpaper and fabrics appeared. The possibilities are unlimited.

While construction was taking place, I taught formal lessons on topics that I thought were important for all students to know. For example, I taught several lessons relating to Thomas Jefferson. We connected the Jefferson Memorial and the National Archives with the Declaration of Independence and the Bill of Rights. We moved forward through his presidency, his scientific interests and inventions at Monticello, his contributions to art and architecture, and his lasting influence on our country.

Students were easily excited about the construction and eager to begin work. However, a great deal of preliminary thinking, planning, and observing took place before the first cutting and gluing began. Likewise, not all construction began at the same time. Students don't all work at the same rate, and they shouldn't be expected to. Some were ready to begin before others, and many different tasks were occurring at the same time.

For example, Eric and Robert might have been working together figuring a pattern for the walls and roof of one of their buildings. At the same time, Cindy and Mary compared notes on the Lincoln Memorial and Ford's Theater and marveled over the interdependence of their two buildings and the complexities of the life and times of Abraham Lincoln. Four other students were discussing how to make columns for their buildings—the White House, the Supreme Court, the Jefferson Memorial, and the Custis-Lee mansion. Meanwhile, I was showing Melody possibilities for measuring the walls of the Capitol. And I'll be truthful; Jake and April were rolling up balls of clay for projectiles to shoot at each other.

You don't want to personally measure walls, make domes, or whatever, but you do want to help your students think through their tasks. Show them different methods for making a building, then let them make their own decisions on what methods to use. Remember that this is the students' city. Not everything will be perfect, but so what—how else does anyone learn except through experimenting? If you really wanted to construct a project to perfection, you'd need to do it in the quiet of your own home without thirty children buzzing about.

Getting the students started How does a teacher guide a student to begin making a building? Beginnings are important and fragile. For some students, a beginning is that moment of high hope mingling with butterflies in the stomach. It may be an almost magical combination—wonderful expectations and nagging doubts. You want your students to see that the beginning of a new endeavor is something special, something to look forward to.

Some students are reluctant to begin anything new, and they must be encouraged in small steps that lead to early successes. The beginning should induce excitement, but also the knowledge that there are many twists and turns, and probably some disappointments. Students should be shown that it is always worth the try to learn and grow.

Students must learn how to plan. First the idea must take shape, and then the plan follows. Materials and tools must be found. Students seem amazed that the work moves ahead in a series of small steps, each dependent on the one before it, steps that are sequential and build upon one another. Obviously they can't build the roof without the walls. Students see the cumulative effect of slow, steady work, and in later life, they can use these lessons on larger projects such as marriage, raising a family, or getting a new job.

Steps for students to follow I offer the following steps for students to follow in planning their buildings:

1. Collect as many pictures as possible that have to do with the building. (I run off things of interest that I have in my collection and put these in a packet for each student. This gets them started and helps build excitement at the beginning.)
2. Read as much as possible about the building, history, people, and anything else that has to do with it.
3. Find the location of the building on a map. Learn about the geography of the building.
4. Ask the question, "When I build this building, what features distinguish it from other structures and buildings?"
5. Decide on the materials to be used—cardboard, paper boxes, PVC pipe, modeling clay, graham crackers and frosting, sugar cubes, styrofoam, paint, wire, twigs, dowels, wallpaper, fabric, and anything else you can use.
6. Decide if the roof should be removable. Ask, "If I design a removable roof, what is important enough to put inside my building?"

Each step offers a fine opportunity for learning. Students should be encouraged to ask such questions as: Is the idea workable? Is it within my capacity? Can I get the right materials?

Reflecting on the outcomes   Many students want to rush into construction without any thought of the sequential steps involved. This may be a result of not understanding the process, or it could be a result of our culture and schooling. Society places too much emphasis on the final product and generally ignores the processes that created the product. The modern world praises any process that is fast, efficient, and cheap. As a result, many children assume that their work should be quick and easy.

Producing a worthwhile product requires thinking and creating. It is a really important outcome of the class project to experience the process of thinking, planning, and then creating. Process—the pleasure of doing and creating—should be the most rewarding part of the work.

It is entirely possible that a building meant to be the most beautiful cathedral in the world—with spires, gargoyles, and stained glass windows—appears (to the spectator) as an ordinary box with some funny looking creatures and messy colored squares glued to its sides. But there is nothing wrong with that if the student learned a lot, feels good about accomplishing something, and is eager to try a new task because the process was an enjoyable creative endeavor.

Students must be able to make mistakes and know that these are part of learning. I wouldn't dream of punishing students or making them feel inadequate because of their mistakes. We do a lot of trying something, deciding it isn't quite what we had in mind, and reworking it or starting over. This takes time, but it is important not to rush the process, or else only a little learning can take place.

For example, a student might paint his or her building and then find that the building has cracked because of the kind of material used. This means trying something else. I have found that if students understand that they can make mistakes when they are learning, they are eager to try again.

In the beginning, I see many students become fearful when something isn't right on the first attempt. We soon get over that hurdle, but it is something I have to teach. I want my students left with a legacy to carry them through life—the idea that a person grows from one small idea to the next, and that eventually their dream (in this case a building) will flourish into reality. That first small idea may be how to make a dome or cut a wall. If these ideas collapse, new ones must be imagined and constructed.

When a student wants to rework something that he or she is unhappy with, and needs guidance, it creates a wonderful opportunity for teachers to "meta" with the student. I am referring to metacognition, thinking about thinking, and talking about how we think and learn. This is a valuable technique to model for your students.

For example, if a student is having trouble cutting a wall, I might ask him or her to describe the problem and explain why he or she decided on that approach. The student's answers will help both of us examine the sequence of thinking that went into the problem. From this point on, I will help the student talk about the problem and his or her thinking—a kind of messing around with ideas—and try to stimulate new lines of thought.

How wonderful to have that student race in the next day shouting, "Guess what, I figured it out last night all by myself!" This is a true learning experience, and one I hope all of our students can shout about. An integrated curriculum opens up many such opportunities.

Always teach your students to observe. Pestalozzi's first principle was to teach children to observe with all of their senses. Could it be that we all underrate and underdevelop our senses throughout the school years and our lifetimes, as Pestalozzi believed? An integrated project is ideal for honing these observational skills.

Students can study the details of their buildings and make sketches of these details. They can measure, draw, and estimate. Thus they will grow in the power of observation. Too often they have been taught the opposite, that if they finish quickly, they can go out to recess or can work on the computer. Hurry, hurry, hurry is the message we often give. How does one observe and hurry?

Making rules that most of us can live with   The classroom is full of eager student architects and construction personnel at work with glue guns, paint, and exacto knives. As much as I hate to admit it, there are times when students aren't on task. But then, what's new? That happens even if they are all doing a worksheet on suffixes. How do you minimize inappropriate behavior (such as fifth graders acting like ten-year-olds)? You and the students must make some rules to live by. Here are some that I have found necessary:

1. **Never use a cutting tool without an adult present.** These tools were kept in my desk, and I accompanied them wherever they went. Students must have guidance with tools.

2. **Handle paint carefully. The lid must be on whenever you are not using it. Always place paper or cardboard under whatever you are painting.** Occasionally a bit of paint might land where it doesn't belong. You must make it clear that the over-enthusiastic Picasso will then clean up the mess.

3. **Only use glue guns with an adult present.** They seem to hold a fascination for students, and if you don't supervise, the hot stuff can be anywhere you don't want it.

4. **Clean up your own mess.** It is helpful to have the class dream up a catchy slogan about cleaning up. With this kind of ownership, students tend to remind others when they leave a mess.

5. **Talk quietly.** I found after listening unobtrusively that most of the student talk is about what the students are doing. They help each other and pass on information that I want them to be familiar with, helping us achieve our goals. But you do need this rule just in case the talk is too loud, about the opposite sex, or about last night's TV program.

6. **Learn to share space, time, and tools.** Each person needs a spot for his or her project, and it must be clear that no one is to disturb someone else's work or materials.

7. **Don't all try to build at the same time.** Even if the student is dying to get his or her hands on a glue gun and get to work, turns must be taken. While some are building, some are researching or figuring out their designs, and others are reading or studying the material, or yes, even just thinking—a skill we don't give enough time for. Many students find they like to have time just to think.

I found it very effective to model the behavior that I expected. We took a couple of days to role play the rules, and it pays off. Of course, when someone breaks a rule, he or she must accept the consequences.

My experience with the students was always positive. At first, there were those who weren't attending their task and wanted to see what they could get away with. Soon, however, these students were caught up in the spirit of things, and they got too involved to misbehave. An esprit de corps builds up as a class focuses on the quest for learning. I always had fewer management problems when I taught this way.

Were there any deadlines? I wanted to give students a sense of unhurried involvement so they could become engrossed in discovery and accomplishment. Eventually, of course, the time came for the culmination of the project. I never set the date until I could see the progress of the class. Your sense of timing and pacing will be your best judge. Don't name the culmination date too far ahead; when the class is nearing completion of the city, set the date for two or three weeks in the future.

Using Volunteers to Help with the Project

Active teaching attracts attention, and I have always been besieged with parents and other people wanting to volunteer. Boise has a long-standing tradition of using parent volunteers; the community expects it.

For the first few years, my students and I worked together on the project without outside help. Since we were successful, we became known, and once people noticed that active learning was in progress, they wanted to help. Most of the volunteers were mothers—artists, organizers, empathizers—all with different talents and willing to give time to kids. Whatever the mix of talent and energy, we always built a fine city.

If you direct the project completely by yourself, things are a little more relaxed because you are setting the pace. However, using volunteers helps create a sense of community with people working together. This is an excellent point to model for students, who see us thinking together and making plans. Students need to see how adults think.

I have conducted the project with and without using volunteers. Both ways were successful. If you have volunteers who agree with your philosophy, it is a wonderful experience, which I have always found to be the case. I don't know whether it was luck or natural selection, but you must decide for yourself whether or not to use volunteers.

I advise you to develop your project for two or three years alone before accepting help from the community. You don't want to be fumbling around in front of volunteers, and you will make plenty of mistakes that you don't want broadcast. One often hears horror stories about the classroom volunteer who talks too much, exaggerates classroom incidents, or reports classroom happenings out of context. If that is a concern of yours, then do the project yourself. Nonetheless, I had wonderful people helping me and didn't have such problems, and I will attest to the fact that volunteers can be wonderful help. My volunteers have been people interested in guiding students through the process of learning. The following three sketches illustrate the kinds of volunteers who found their way into my classroom.

Carol Sayers Carol held a degree in art. She delighted in analytical thinking and prodding the students into thinking. Carol was the first person I saw actively use metacognition with learners. Neither of us had ever heard of the word at the time, but she knew it worked, and I did too after observing her. This is a case of not knowing the ivory tower vocabulary, but using the method because it worked. You have probably had similar experiences.

Carol was a genius on thinking through the steps of designing and constructing a building. She would talk it through so that students could observe the problem-solving process. Carol didn't just stop with one idea, but often suggested several ways to solve a problem. These were valuable insights for the students. How often do we orally communicate how we solve a problem? In most cases, not often enough.

Carol also loved to show students how to begin research for interesting information. Again they could observe her on the trail for information. Before long, they would emulate her research skills.

Of course, her artistic talent was invaluable. Carol would show a student how to mix the right color of paint, or how to make the outside of Petersen House (the house where Lincoln died) look like bricks. This is what students need to see and then do for themselves; it provides an integrity for learning. With this kind of modeling, it is hard for a student not to become an independent learner—because the pleasure of using the mind becomes an intrinsic value.

Another advantage of working with people like Carol is that I also learned a lot. We were all inspired.

Ted's Mom   You never know what name the students will use to address you or the volunteer. One year, Ted's mother was the project volunteer. Whenever she appeared, someone would say, "There's Ted's Mom!" Ted's Mom was also an artist. She would come almost every day, put on her work apron, and help several students with their projects. She had wonderful ideas for taking something ordinary like a bottle cap and turning it into something inventive.

Ted's Mom showed students how to rework something if they were unhappy with their progress. They learned that a failed try was a necessary concomitant to discovery. They learned that successful students probably have more mistakes to their credit than unsuccessful students—because they try more things. Before long, the students who had been afraid to make mistakes understood that it was okay to try out an idea, then rethink and redesign. These are lessons many adults have never learned, ones far more important to me than learning that the Lincoln Memorial has thirty-six columns.

Joyce Sherman   Joyce Sherman was a dedicated volunteer who demonstrated a great sensitivity for helping students reach their potential. All children should experience someone like Joyce. She was also extremely well organized, and at the end of her volunteer experience she developed guidelines to assist future volunteers. Here are her guidelines.

Welcome to the wonderful world of construction! You are about to enter into the realm of cardboard, masking tape, hot glue, and poster paint. When you emerge on the completed side of Washington, DC, you will have the knowledge that you have accomplished a great thing. You will have built an entire nation's capital! You may also rest assured that this feat will settle in your mind, forever, your concept of yourself as a volunteer.

I have attempted to summarize the Washington experience, emphasizing the areas I found to be troublesome. I hope this will assist you in your efforts.

1. *Scale:* The scale of the buildings is fairly loose. You will find it easier to look at the largest and the smallest, set their sizes as the standard, and then gauge all others somewhere between the two.

   Largest: U.S. Capitol—approximately 3' × 2' × 3'
   Tallest: Washington Monument—approximately 1' × 1' × 5'
   Smallest: Vice President's house—approximately 8" × 8" × 8"
   House where Lincoln died—approximately 5" × 7" × 10"

2. *Timing:* Planning is absolutely crucial to the quality, success, and sanity of this project. I highly recommend the use of a chart. This would enable all involved to monitor his or her progress. You accomplish this by first establishing the "finish date." Then working backward, you schedule who will start working at what date, based on the difficulty of the building and when the work needs to be completed. You have to stagger "start and stop" times, because all of the students cannot work at once.

This method would solve another problem less visible than getting done on time—making sure everyone has a turn. This problem is two-fold. First, some of the students will burst forward, full of enthusiasm and energy and will work hard to complete their buildings. Some will leap to the forefront in the same manner and never get done! Both groups will, more likely than not, take most of your time. They are aggressive, and you can get caught up in their enthusiasm.

In the meantime, there is a quiet group of students who will sit back and wait for a turn, wishing to get a chance to build, and silently feeling rejected because they always were ignored or put off until another time.

By charting who starts when, and who needs to be done when, you have given yourself and the students a "map" and a "date," thereby harnessing some students who would wildly control you the entire time, motivating others who can stretch out the smallest job into weeks of unending business (always working, never finishing), and giving the quiet ones equal opportunity and access to a very special event.

3. *Supplies:* The supplies you will need are easily obtainable. They will come from the school, the kids' homes, the store, and trash dumpsters. Use your judgment and contacts for everything, keeping in mind that this should not be a financial drain on the students' parents. You wouldn't want that dollar for glue sticks to be the last dollar a family might have in the house. You will need:

cardboard boxes (all sizes)	clay (homemade play dough)
masking tape	fabric remnants
Elmer's Glue	clothes pins
construction paper	razor blade cutters
wallpaper samples or rolls	scissors
felt squares	colored tissue paper
paint	twigs
carpet samples or remnants	bleach bottles
PVC pipe	moss
styrofoam balls	beads
flags	
toothpicks	

and anything else you or the student can think of to make the building both authentic and decorative.

One last comment on the supplies. Many of the kids are unfamiliar with craft tools and supplies. They like to play with them just for the fun of it. This can be very wasteful and expensive. Tell them at the beginning what you expect and what you won't allow! Then, if someone uses up a pile of glue sticks in play, he or she will know who is responsible to replace them.

My last comment on this project is to encourage you to be patient. Keep in mind that when you are tired and frustrated, you still have a fragile self-esteem in the palm of your hand, and you don't want to damage anyone by making him or her feel small or inadequate, even though that might be true at the moment.

You will leave this project with friends, love, and a knowledge that you have made a difference in someone's life.

Have fun! This is going to be one of your best experiences ever!

How could anyone go wrong with assistants like these! And they are only three of the many I could have described. They illustrate the wonderful talent and resources available to our classrooms. When I start thinking about the many people who have volunteered their time to me and my students, I am amazed at how much dedication and love these people give. Every volunteer brought an individual viewpoint and his or her own particular set of skills and enriched the lives of my students, not to mention my own life. We all experienced a true sense of community and personal enrichment. I hope that when my students are adults, they will reflect back on these wonderful people and be inspired to serve their own communities.

3

Designing and Planning the Latin America Project

I remember reading my slip of paper. It simply read "Guano Islands." "Guano Islands?" I questioned. "I don't even know where that is." I was soon to learn that the where *wasn't as important as the* what. *Islands covered with bird droppings! It was gross and I loved it. I had great fun dreaming up ways to accurately portray such a thing.*

— Shauri Sluder, former student

*A*fter several years of teaching fifth grade and spreading Washington, DC, all over the floor, I moved to sixth grade and began spreading Latin America all over the floor. Different content, same idea. The project format still worked!

The room erupted into life and color from the blue Caribbean and the mysterious Bermuda Triangle to Tierra del Fuego and the frozen tip of Antarctica. Each country, cut from a different color of butcher paper, vied for attention. The Andes, that giant ridge of mountains rising thousands of feet above the sea, seemed to reach for the sky. The Amazon Basin spread its canopy of green from the Andes to the Atlantic. Further south, woolly sheep grazed contentedly on the shimmering Pampa.

The Western Hemisphere is the prescribed focus for sixth-grade social studies in Idaho and a number of other states. This follows naturally from the study of the United States in fifth grade, and the study of state history/social studies in fourth grade. Though sixth graders study both Canada and Latin America, Latin America is the greater focus in our school system. I also think it has much greater potential for a fascinating class project because it contains such a variety of cultures and countries.

People often ask me which project I preferred, Washington, DC, or Latin America. The answer is whichever one I was involved with at the time. Washington, DC, is very geometric and monochromatic, since most of the buildings are white. One principal even ordered cases of white tempera paint for me. Washington, DC, is very symbolic and awe inspiring. Parents identify with it readily; many have taken their children there after the project. Latin America, however, seems to explode in color and energy, giving a sense of the wonderful things that can be learned about our world. Whatever I was teaching and learning with children, I became totally focused and engaged and liked it best.

These differences, however, are merely cosmetic. Beneath them lie essential differences in the scope of the projects and the frameworks that guided them. The Washington, DC, project was organized around the nation's capital and its symbols. This gave the project a certain sense of convergence. Though the project contained elements of the six strands of social studies, they were not the organizing principle.

By contrast, the Latin America project was organized systematically along the six strands of social studies. In addition, it offered more divergence through the study of many countries and cultures and an almost infinite choice of subject matter. Washington, DC, and Latin America provide the teacher with two case studies, each illustrating a different way of organizing and focusing a class project.

As with Washington, DC, the Latin America project was never the same twice. Though many of the strands remained the same each year, history and changing times altered the project. One election year, the sign "Where's the Beef?" was erected in Argentina. Ordinarily, this wouldn't carry much humor or significance, but at the time, this was a U.S. political slogan based on a popular TV fast-food commercial. Another year, a student built an English ship dashing through Atlantic waves to the Falkland Islands with Margaret Thatcher as the figurehead. This was during the Falkland War between Argentina and Great Britain, and Margaret Thatcher was the British Prime Minister.

The study of Latin America is an ideal opportunity to help our students understand other cultures. This understanding is imperative today if we are to interpret the world around us accurately, and to understand the rapid cultural changes taking place in our own country.

Creating a Latin American Tapestry

What did we use to create our world of Latin America? Just as Latin America erupts with life and color, so it also erupts with shapes and images, history and geography, ideas and culture, fact and fiction. One can weave an infinite number of differing tapestries by choosing from an endless number of strands of different colors and textures, given the diversity in Latin America. Following are examples of some of the people and places, flora and fauna, places and events that provided strands. The choice of tapestry is yours.

Bahamas	Llamas
Bermuda Triangle	Quito
Lesser and Greater Antilles	Lake Titicaca
Monroe Doctrine	Andrew Selkirk
Veracruz	Dr. Carlos Finlay
Maya	Daniel Defoe's Imaginary Island
Inca	Aedes aegypti
Aztec	Robinson Crusoe and Friday
Montezuma	Galapagos Islands
Cortés	Polynesia
Conquistadors	Columbus
Rio de Janeiro	Magellan
Buenos Aires	Strait of Magellan
Angel Falls	El Dorado
Sugar Loaf Mountain	Hacienda
Cusco	Popocatepetl
Machu Picchu	Isthmus of Panama
Amazon River Basin	Patagonian Express

Balsam of Peru

Diego Rivera

San Martin

Toussaint L'Ouverture

Pizarro

Open Pit Copper Mine

Sugar Cane

Atacama Desert

Andes Mountains

Cape Horn

Pampa

Amazon Rain Forest

Orinoco River People

Panama Hat

Cacao

Plantations

Thor Heyerdahl

Peru Current or Humboldt
  Current

Easter Island

Guano

Tin Mines

Gatun Lake

Blackbeard

Captain Kidd

Christ of the Andes

Patagonia

Gaucho

Brasília

Simón Bolívar

Coffee Plantation

Bernardo O'Higgins

Morelas

Atahualpa

Iturbide

São Paulo

Machete

Cassava

Chicle

Mahogany

Bananas

Mexico City

Tenochtitlán

Lake Maracaibo

Falkland Islands

Kapok

Panama Canal and the Locks

Henequen

Yerba Maté

Trinidad

Tobago

Grenada

Santiago

Sisal

Devil's Island

Captain Dreyfus

Birds and Animals

Tip of Antarctica

Hispaniola

Argentina beef

Venezuelan oil

These were not just words; they became a total environment. Imagine all of these words as images spread across the floor. Imagine students involved in numerous conversations about them. Visualize the color, the beauty, and the intermingling of centuries of ideas and people that were recreated by a sixth-grade class—a multicultural milieu. Observe the connectivity and relationships students made and discovered about themselves and others. See students beginning to understand how diversity adds richness to life.

The students learned through experiencing, reading, discussing, creating, making mistakes, and thinking. They measured, glued, read, researched, and wrote about their ideas. The project focused on the people, events, plants, animals, and interactions that took place over several centuries. As before, resources were provided for the students, and often volunteers joined in our group learning. But the students made it all happen!

Planning and Organizing the Project

The planning process for the Latin America project was exactly the same as for Washington, DC. The project began in January, drawing upon learnings begun in September. Research and construction continued until May and were culminated with Tour Day. Students were eager and excited about Latin America, just as they had been with Washington, DC.

Building such a project was not a single act, nor a simple step-by-step process. Many activities were going on at the same time, with different students doing different things—studying, researching, sketching, planning, learning, gathering materials, rethinking, starting over, thinking again, gathering new insights, and making sense out of it all. And while construction was taking place, I taught formal lessons on topics that I thought were important for all students to know.

It seemed logical to begin with the three greatest Indian civilizations of Latin America and work forward in time. Thus we began in September with a study of the Maya, Inca, and Aztec Indians. These learnings were in place when the project began in January, so we could start adding new layers beginning with the Indians' encounters with European explorers.

The Maya, Aztec, and Inca were three important pieces of the total Latin America project, and students delighted in constructing the Indians' cities, monuments, and farms. The Indians' history, much of it revealed through their monuments, naturally led students to consider how geography influenced the Indians' social, political, and economic systems. Native American culture was part of the fifth-grade study of the United States, but the students were greatly surprised at the sophistication of the Indian civilizations of Latin America.

The students' understanding of the Indian cultures was sharpened by the cultural contrasts that followed the Indians' encounters with the European explorers, beginning with Columbus and continuing with other Europeans, particularly the Spaniards. This aspect of Latin American history connected nicely with fifth-grade social studies, for the arrival of Columbus in America started the European influx that eventually led to the settlement of the North American colonies.

The shape of each country of Latin America was cut from a different color of butcher paper and placed on the floor, creating a giant jigsaw puzzle. Students traced the countries from a map projected on the wall. Tracing and cutting provided valuable experience in working with materials, shapes, and spatial relationships. Additional parts of the project included constructing mountain ranges, lakes, cities, and other features, which were then spread across the map. Walking daily around the map on the floor reinforced the students' sense of the shape, distance, and juxtaposition of countries and geographic features.

Making Curriculum Choices

Latin America is a perfect curriculum for integrating all six strands of social studies: history, geography, government, economics, sociology, and anthropology. Appendix B describes these six strands in detail. Latin America also provides rich opportunities for integrating other sixth-grade subjects—reading, writing, science, math, art, music, and theater. We integrated these other subjects with the same techniques and strategies used with the Washington, DC, project.

The six strands of social studies provide a solid rationale for making curriculum choices. Latin America is so huge, sprawling, and diverse, that choosing what to teach is a challenge. With its many countries, cultures, and impossibly varied landscape, one can only sample its offerings. Choices of specific subject matter may seem arbitrary, but we can't go far wrong building upon the required social studies curriculum and the six strands of social studies.

The six strands must be integrated—woven into a single curriculum—rather than being studied as separate subjects. As the teacher, I identified broad topics and concepts to be learned. And as co-learners, the students and I identified interesting—often fascinating—information to work with. As the students got involved in the project, they usually found more areas they wanted to pursue.

History encompasses drama, vibrancy, legends, heroes, and narrative stories—the flesh and blood of the past. The story of people, however, has to happen somewhere, in a social setting, within a particular culture, and for some reason. Thus history is a definable part of, but inseparable from, the other strands of social studies. Other areas of the curriculum such as language arts, science, music, and art can be used to invigorate the drama.

Historical issues add spice to the drama of history, and they also invite students to engage in inquiry and critical thinking. Students need to learn that history has more than one set of interpretations, and that different groups of people place different interpretations on the same event. A striking example is the controversy over the arrival of Columbus in America. Did he *discover* America, or is there a better description of his arrival? What impact did the arrival of the Spaniards have on America?

Sociology and anthropology are inescapably part of the drama of history. Sociology is the study of groups of people and the interactions of these groups, while anthropology is the study of people's culture and institutions. Through the human dramas of history, students get to look at people's beliefs and behavior, how they choose to live together, and how they make war. Students also see that through the use of imagination and inventiveness, people have devised ways of growing and manufacturing, bartering and trading, reading and writing, communicating and traveling, and governing one another. Thus the study of history also involves the study of geography, government, and economics.

Too often, students groan at the mention of geography because they associate geography with memory work. Contemporary geography, however, is studied around the Five Themes of Geography, which are described in Appendix B. Thus students study not only location and place, but also the movement of people, goods, and ideas; the interaction of people with their environment; and the region in which they themselves live.

In geography too, controversial issues can add zest. What should be done about the Amazon rain forest? What should be done about urban sprawl? How can a country protect itself from pollution produced in another country? These are issues that people face everywhere, including here in our own country. These issues make the study of geography seem highly relevant to students.

The material described in this chapter represents a panorama of people, places, and events that can stir students' imaginations. It is up to us, the teachers, to engage our students in those visions and feelings to bring social studies alive. There is no better subject matter to accomplish this than Latin America.

Student Questing—A Key to Integration

The quests of students often have unexpected results. The Latin America project was no exception; in fact, it seemed to generate more than its fair share of success stories. Those success stories have helped me to understand how learning occurs and what is important in a classroom. We may become more expert in learning theory by analyzing how learning is occurring in our classrooms.

A professor receives an education

Before embarking on the Latin America project, we studied the Aztec, the Maya, and the Inca Indians. One year, I learned about a local university professor whose specialty was Aztec, Mayan, and Incan culture. He agreed—very reluctantly—to come to our class, although he said he knew very little about children.

The students were excited to have an "expert" coming who could answer their questions and lead them to other insights. As they studied these three cultures, the students collected interesting questions to ask the professor during his visit. When they seemed to have enough background, the professor came.

The nervous professor arrived ready to give a lecture. No sooner had he started his lecture when a forest of student hands went up. The questioning had begun! This was something he had not expected, and at first he was flustered at being distracted from his lecture. Within a few minutes, however, the professor got over his nervousness and began to enjoy the dialogue. He expanded and gained enthusiasm. He never got back to his lecture, and no lecture was needed. Instead of the hour that he had planned, he stayed all morning, and we were all disappointed when he had to leave. There were still more things to talk about! An exhausted and invigorated professor had learned a lot about students that day.

Before leaving, the professor spent a few minutes talking with me. He was astounded that sixth graders had such curiosity and joy of learning. He was amazed at the knowledge they had acquired, the depth of what they knew, and their ability to develop rudimentary theories and to speculate. What had happened, he wanted to know, to his university students, who merely sat?

The second year, the professor planned to stay all morning. This time, he brought books and slides to share with the students. The third year, he brought his wife, who needed proof that sixth graders could be enthusiastic learners, ask thoughtful questions, and possess so much information.

One year a student came up with a question that the professor had never thought of, and the professor was off on a new tack. The student had even uncovered some valuable information for the professor. Can you imagine the effect on a group of sixth graders when a professor tells them that they have taught him some new things about Latin America? This, of course, was a tremendous motivator for the students, and it caused a flurry of digging for new information.

Our experiences with the professor illustrate that we had truly become a learning community, one that included the professor, the teacher, the students, and their parents. Now we were ready for other quests—quests leading to the construction of Latin America.

The stories that follow illustrate the varied responses and learnings of individual students. We see students who suddenly discovered learning, got caught up in problem solving and decision making, and discovered new talents. The students were involved in open-ended activities that they could pursue in any direction they chose and at whatever depth they chose. Within the limits of the curriculum, they could quest to their hearts' content.

Carol engineers the Panama Canal

Carol drew the Panama Canal from the hat, and it changed her life— she told me this years later when I met her and her baby at the mall. Carol was an uninterested student until she got caught up in constructing the Panama Canal. Somehow the functioning of the locks intrigued her, so she and her mother set off for the Boise Public Library, where they checked out all the books anyone could want to read about the Panama Canal. Then Carol began building the canal, the locks, and anything else she felt was related. By the time she was finished, she had a huge paper mosquito hanging from the ceiling, hovering over the entire operation.

The Panama Canal was one of the great engineering achievements of the world—for the original engineers, for the workers, and for Carol. Carol obviously used different materials than the engineers did, but the result was just as magnificent to us. She used cardboard for the locks, and constructed different levels, with ships easing through. The areas representing the water were painted blue. Before Carol was finished, *the Gatun Locks, the Gaillard Locks, the Pedro Miguel Locks, the Miraflores Locks, De Lesseps,* and *cubic meters* were all part of her everyday vocabulary. She had integrated science, mathematics, social studies, reading, writing, researching, and art in her work—all because she was interested and her quest led her in these directions. Carol could discuss her work at a very high level. By Tour Day, Carol was not only an expert on the Panama Canal, but had become an independent learner full of excitement and confidence in her own ability.

Rosalie and the Amazon Basin

One year, the entire Amazon Basin and rain forest was alive and well in our classroom. One student, Rosalie, had taken special pride in planning and organizing the project. Rather than merely using crepe paper, a favorite in previous years, Rosalie diligently sought out a variety of small, live plants that she crafted into a believable rain forest. Her Amazon Basin was resplendent with live greenery. She then added models of people and animals. Each day, she carefully watered the rain forest.

After Tour Day, Rosalie began taking away a few plants every day, changing the atmosphere of the rain forest from lush and vibrant to bare and muddy in just a few days. When classmates asked Rosalie what she was doing, she told them that she was selling her plants to people who wanted them. At first the other students objected to this, for they had become proud of their Amazon rain forest. But Rosalie was making a point, and soon the other students understood.

Through the research involved for her project, Rosalie had become involved in a controversial issue with worldwide implications. Her quest had led her into the intricacies of nature and the complexity of the tropical rain forest issue. Though she read articles on both sides of the issue, she became highly concerned that the Amazon rain forest was being destroyed. Through the calculated destruction of her own rain forest, she captured the interest and involvement of others. As the project ended, spirited discussions were in full swing.

Todd conquers the Andes The challenge of building the Andes involved calculating the height of the peaks and the depth of the valleys. Todd was especially intrigued by the problem of accuracy. He pondered the atlas, especially the chart of mountain peaks. On butcher paper, he drew an enlarged version of the chart—fifteen feet long! Then, using his enlarged chart, he began carefully crafting chicken wire into mountains, peaks, and valleys. The result was a mountain range with the tallest peak in the right place, and the other peaks and valleys in their proper places and relationships.

Todd then covered the chicken wire with a large blanket of "drip and drape," a product made of strips of cloth impregnated with plaster of paris, which hardens after being dipped in water. Thus he transformed the skeletal Andes into a ghostly mountain range. After the mountains had hardened, Todd used a final coat of brown and white tempera to bring the magnificent Andes into full view. The result was a truly remarkable mountain range dominating the South American continent. Todd's model of the Andes was the backbone of Latin America. (For several years thereafter, it decorated a wall in my garage.)

Other students would watch Todd at work, fascinated with his problem-solving process. They would talk about what he was doing and ask him questions. Todd loved to explain his work and took pride in describing how he had figured out what to do. Thus the other students gained insights from watching a creation take place, learning from the modeling of both thought and action—experiencing metacognition before I even knew the word. The students even learned what chicken wire was, for few of them had ever seen a live chicken, let alone a chicken farm. And the other students were astonished at what a classmate had accomplished.

Shauri and the guano islands

Students have consistently been amazed and fascinated by the story of guano and the guano islands of Peru. At one time, some of the islands were covered with more than one hundred feet of guano (sea bird and bat droppings), which was mined for fertilizer. The guano fertilizer was used by farmers in Peru. While guano, at first glance, may not seem to be a particularly significant topic for the study of Latin America, it is one of those very interesting and unique anomalies that fascinate children. Intense interest in one topic leads easily into another.

Shauri was astounded to learn about the guano islands. She started out expecting to find some uninteresting islands on a map but, as she later noted, "was soon to learn that the *where* wasn't as important as the *what.*" The topic has just the right degree of mild grossness to fascinate children, and this unexpected turn was the "hook" that captured Shauri.

Shauri's guano islands served as the base for other discoveries. She discovered geography and economics: guano had long been mined, transported, and sold to farmers for fertilizer, thus producing jobs and increasing the productivity of farms. What better way than a project like this to make geography and economics interesting?

Jamie finds Robinson Crusoe

Did you know that the story of Robinson Crusoe was inspired by a true adventure? Neither do most children. In the 1700s, Alexander Selkirk, a hot-tempered sailor, was put off of a ship on a distant, lonely island far off the coast of Chile. Selkirk spent four years on that island before he was rescued by a passing ship. Meanwhile, he had fed and sheltered himself on the island, where he was reduced to wearing goat skins. Daniel DeFoe used Selkirk as a model for Robinson Crusoe, changing many details and moving the island into the Caribbean Sea off the coast of Venezuela.

I read *Robinson Crusoe* aloud to the class during the Latin America project, and students were spellbound by the story. One year, Jamie drew "Robinson Crusoe" from the hat. He researched the location of both islands (DeFoe's was fictional), constructed them from butcher paper, and placed them on the floor. Later, he added details to each island—models of trees, goats, huts, and people.

Having run out of things to add to his islands, Jamie decided to put on a Robinson Crusoe play. He wrote a script, recruited a cast, built props, and held practices. Then the cast sent invitations to parents, requesting that the parents read *Robinson Crusoe* before they came to the play. Of course, the play was held on Friday, and it was a great success!

While *Robinson Crusoe* may not immediately seem important to the study of Latin America, it served as a vehicle for several important learnings. It helped teach geography, emphasizing location, climate, resources, and history. In addition, it integrated literature into social studies, and demonstrated the self-sufficiency of Alexander Selkirk, Robinson Crusoe—and Jamie! Last but not least, it provided valuable experiences for students in writing, thinking, acting, and self-expression.

Amanda and the Spanish-speaking macaw

Most of my students had seen parrots at one time or another. They were interested to learn that there are about 315 species of parrot, and that about half of these live in Latin America. Amanda liked to visit a certain parrot at a local pet shop, a large, colorful scarlet macaw that greeted her with "Hi, Sweetie." Of course, the bird repeated the phrase over and over, and said little else. During one visit to the pet shop, Amanda learned that the parrot had come from Mexico. "Then maybe it speaks Spanish," she said.

Amanda didn't know any Spanish, so she asked someone working at the pet shop whether the parrot "spoke" Spanish. No one at the shop knew the answer, because none of them understood Spanish, either. The next day, she asked her classmates how she could find out whether her parrot friend knew any Spanish words.

There were no Spanish-speaking families in our school, so none of the other students could help her. Finally, Brandi remembered that her brother, Mark, a high school student, was taking Spanish. Even though Brandi said, "He isn't very good at it," she volunteered her brother.

Amanda, Brandi, and Mark arranged to visit the pet shop together. Mark greeted the parrot with "buenos días." "Buenos días, buenos días, buenos días, buenos días," the parrot repeated. He began hopping about excitedly on his perch, and suddenly leaped to Mark's shoulder.

"Buenos días, buenos días, buenos días." The bird began searching Mark's shirt pocket, apparently for food. When the shopkeeper heard the racket, she came over and rescued Mark from the parrot.

When Amanda and Brandi told their story to the class, the students were greatly interested. Someone suggested that we needed a parrot for our project. Several students volunteered to make parrots out of construction paper, and soon the room began to fill with colorful paper parrots of many shades, shapes, and sizes. They hung from the bulletin board, the window shades, and the light fixtures. Amanda, with her usual flair, created a life-sized macaw in brilliant hues of orange, yellow, green, and blue, and stood it on a perch in the middle of Mexico. Below it she placed a sign: "Buenos Días."

Brad and life after Latin America

On a recent summer day, I was buying paint and discovered that the clerk who waited on me was Brad, a student I'd taught fifteen years earlier. He recognized me and proceeded to fill me in on some of his life since school. Not only had he traveled extensively throughout Latin America, fulfilling a dream sparked in sixth grade, but he also had just reread *Kon-Tiki*. In fact, he said he had read all of Heyerdahl's books after he became hooked on Heyerdahl in sixth grade.

I always read books to my students, especially those that brought life to our study of Latin America. *Kon-Tiki*, by Thor Heyerdahl, was a favorite. This story is about the true adventure of Heyerdahl and five other men on a small balsa-wood raft, who, in 1947, sailed from Peru to eastern Polynesia across four thousand miles of open sea. Heyerdahl was testing his theory that the Polynesian Islands could have been settled by Indians who sailed from South America.

Heyerdahl, a famed anthropologist, proposed several intriguing but controversial theories that challenged older theories about the movement of peoples. In another book, *Aku-Aku*, Heyerdahl proposed a connection between Easter Island and Latin America. In 1970, he set out to demonstrate that ancient Egyptians could have sailed to the Americas. He and a small crew sailed in a papyrus reed boat, the *Ra-2*, from Morocco in northern Africa to Barbados in the West Indies. Students were intrigued to learn about these possibilities.

Heyerdahl was used in class as a springboard for discussion and critical thinking. His theories were controversial, not the final answers, and students understood this. Students need to confront controversy to prepare them for the adult world. Heyerdahl's ideas led them into a world of speculation and research, a quest for answers, an important step toward becoming informed adults.

Food for Thought

One important theme in the study of Latin America is the foods grown and eaten by the people in those countries. All children in my part of the U.S. are familiar with Mexican food because Mexican food and restaurants are popular. It was a surprise to many students, therefore, to learn that people in other parts of Latin America don't eat Mexican food. From Argentina to Venezuela to Panama to Cuba, countries have their own particular foods, based mainly on the agriculture of their own regions.

Skye was astounded to read that Bolivia grows more than two hundred kinds of potatoes. She had found an article on potatoes, complete with amazing photographs, in an old issue of the *National Geographic*. (In Idaho, we tend to think that all potatoes are Idaho russets.) Clarence was intrigued by the story of chocolate and cacao beans. Russ discovered that the grapes in a local supermarket had come from Chile.

It was a revelation to the students that while Latin America has many unique crops (bananas, mangoes, chocolate, cassava), the people also grow and eat many of the same foods that we grow and eat in the U.S.: beef, pork, chicken, wheat, corn, rice, beans, sugar, grapes, apples, and many others. Thus we moved beyond our previous awareness of tacos, burritos, and enchiladas.

When two of our class volunteers, Mrs. DeMarco and Mrs. McKinley, volunteered to prepare a Latin American meal at lunch time on Tour Day, I was delighted. Latin American food on Tour Day added a flavor of authenticity to the activities of the day. In addition, it provided opportunities for students to make more connections with Latin America.

Food is a uniquely personal experience. It provides a unique kind of communication—a universal connection among people. Eating is most often a social activity and an act of friendship. When integrated into a project, food can be educational as well as nutritional, and it provides one more highlight to a festive occasion.

4

Bridging Abilities

It is impossible to give a proper impression of Ramses by describing his characteristics. One must observe him in action.

— Elizabeth Peters, *The Last Camel Died At Noon*

Students learn in ways that are identifiably distinctive.

— Howard Gardner, *The Unschooled Mind*

*L*ike classrooms all over America, mine contained a mix of personalities and abilities. Brian was brilliant, artistic, and considerate of others. Michelle was cheerful, witty, and a natural leader. Lennie could never stay in his seat for more than sixty seconds. Molly talked constantly, and I got tired of competing with her for air time. Patty was sweet, shy, and read two years below grade level. Kevin had been mainstreamed from the special education program. And there were many others, of course. Just kids—all kinds—a normal classroom.

Often, as the children worked on their projects, the sun shone on them through the windows, giving almost a halo effect. At such times, I marveled that each of us in this collage was creating and producing, alive, animated, and thinking. Each had strengths, weaknesses, and personalities that added depth and richness to the classroom. That included not just a talented few, but everyone!

It is important that we, as teachers, make all our students feel accepted by allowing them to study and work with their own traits and abilities to become what they are capable of being. If students don't learn to use their abilities in the classroom, how will it happen outside of the classroom? Integration means more than just subject matter. It also means integration of personalities, ideas, talents, traits— the bridging of abilities.

Project teaching creates an educational environment where every student is learning and growing in a spirit of acceptance and collegiality. Students of differing abilities work together, gaining knowledge from each other, learning to relate to each other, and being accountable to each other. Project teaching bridges those abilities. It opens up the opportunity for all students to engage in and share their many abilities, and it is truly amazing how many talents come to light if only we are willing to look at learning as more than just one dimensional.

People sometimes asked how it is possible to keep a class project moving when there are so many different special needs to be met. In fact, project teaching meets the special needs of students because they are allowed to be themselves. This becomes apparent as you watch "special needs" children interact with the project and with their peers. These students have given me more wonderful insights and clues to teaching and learning than I have learned from any other source. The following stories illustrate some of those lessons.

Keith's Story

The first time I saw Keith, he stormed into our class carrying his notebook, *The National Inquirer*, and a gigantic chip on his shoulder. He announced that he never began his morning without reading *The National Inquirer,* and proceeded to do just that.

This was our introduction to Keith, who, I soon learned, had just been expelled from another school. He was brilliant, angry, and rebellious, and our previously calm, orderly classroom was changed forever. If it is true that we occasionally need a jolt in our lives to awaken us to new ideas, emotions, language, and talent, then Keith provided us with a truly healthy growth experience. I say this now, looking back. At the time, it was less than appreciated. After all, I already knew that he had mooned the bus driver.

It was mid-year, and we had already started our Latin America project. All of the individual projects had been taken, so it was necessary for Keith and me to find him one. I wanted Keith to make the choice, but for more than a week he refused to show any interest at all. He scornfully watched the other students work on their projects, made slighting remarks about them, and "accidentally" knocked a few things around. The rest of the time, he sat alone and read books.

The time had come to "lean" on Keith, and I did. I made it clear that he would have to participate with the class if he was going to stay in our school. Apparently this made an impression on Keith, or else Bluebeard did, because the next day he announced for anyone to hear that he was going to "do" the Pirates of the Caribbean. He had slyly been reading about pirates when he thought I wasn't looking. I liked his choice, thank goodness, and didn't try to change his mind.

Though somewhat subdued, Keith still subjected us to rebellious tantrums from time to time. We might find someone's torn-up notebook in the wastebasket, or the contents of a desk spilled out on the floor. Occasionally we would be entertained by a deluge of "adult" language. Interestingly, Keith never disturbed anyone else's project. We learned to live with his erratic behavior, and gradually it improved. Soon Keith became intensely involved with his work and spent considerably less time irritating the rest of us.

As I said, Keith was brilliant, and his research, ships, pirates, crossbones, skulls, and stories about pirates were authentic and intriguing. I had to admit that an important piece of the project would have been missing if Keith hadn't invaded our classroom. He added a richness to our study, and provided valuable lessons in tolerance and diversity.

Gerald's Story

Is it possible to integrate a very emotionally disturbed child into a regular classroom? My answer varies from day to day. But I also believe in the moral imperatives of being a teacher: We must not give up on any child, no matter how we are tempted, nor take any shortcuts that negatively affect a child's life. We are not in a shortcut profession.

Gerald's story needs to be told—even though it has many sad and painful chapters. Gerald lived in a very abusive home until his grandparents adopted him and he became part of a loving and caring family. When we met, he carried many emotional scars, perhaps impossible to eradicate.

Gerald was angry, volatile, and destructive, and needed close supervision at all times. The class was building Washington, DC, that year, and combining Gerald with the project was one of the greatest challenges of my career. We were tackling emotional upheaval, not lack of ability, for he was quite clever with his work. We had to find ways around his destructive impulses.

Gerald would unpredictably kick someone, or spit on someone, or throw his scissors. He sometimes stabbed himself with scissors purposely so he could get blood on his work or someone else's. We never knew when a strike would come. To integrate Gerald into the classroom milieu, classmates, volunteers, and I spent endless hours sitting by him, talking to him about his work, and working with him on his project.

Gerald's project was the Air and Space Museum, and in a sense, Gerald became *our* project. Could we help him to find some peace and sense of self? He ultimately became immersed in the planes, rockets, and history of flight, and he loved designing and talking about the many things inside the museum. He developed a building with long Saran Wrap windows that let a viewer, on hands and knees, catch sight of the many artifacts suspended inside.

Guided by our patience and understanding, Gerald found solace and challenge in the Washington, DC, project, and began to develop connections with other people. He still had emotional outbursts, but not so often and not so dramatically. Left to his own way of thinking and doing, he seemed calmer and occasionally was able to work with other students.

Our creating classroom provided space for Gerald and his problems, allowing him to make progress emotionally and intellectually. The absence of rigid guidelines enabled Gerald to engage in his own ways of thinking and creating. He was able to calm down and think about learning. As he engaged in active learning, Gerald shifted some of his thinking to ideas beyond himself.

It was a start. . . .

When I asked Gerald's grandmother to come and work as a volunteer for the class, she did so gladly. I still have vivid images of Gerald's grandmother working with students. On one occasion, she and several students put up butcher paper for a bulletin board to graph animal behavior. Together, they planned, measured, cut, and stapled. I see her yet kneeling on the floor with a glue gun, carefully showing Lee how to use it to connect bridge parts, and sitting at a table helping Brenda build zoo animals.

And what about Gerald? He continued to calm down. The other students became much kinder to him because they liked his grandmother and appreciated her help. Finally, he was able to build his own project and show interest in other students' projects. This helped him become one of the class, not an outsider. He felt proud that his grandmother was part of our esprit de corps.

Gerald's story does not offer a solution to all problems; each child presents a different situation. But Gerald's story, like the others, shows that many different types of students benefit from the educational freedom the project provides.

Mark's Story

One year as I prepared my room before the opening of school, I sat at my desk for a few quiet moments. "I'm tired already," I thought. "This year, I'm not going to build Latin America. We'll just sit calmly in our seats and read the book and answer the questions." I fantasized about my new life. I would be full of energy for activities outside of my school life.

Abruptly I was jolted from my reverie by Mark and his mother, who had just walked into my classroom. "We want the volcano!" announced Mark's mother in a spirited outburst. Poof! With those few words, my wonderful fantasy evaporated. How could I dampen such enthusiasm? Besides, I knew in my heart I couldn't teach any other way.

Mark had coasted through life, all eleven years of it, and was prepared to continue coasting. That was before he became engrossed in his project for Latin America—volcanoes. Yes, Mark, amazingly enough, did draw "volcanoes" from the hat, and the result was extraordinary. His volcano spewed and bubbled above the surrounding countryside of people, flora, and fauna. Given the necessary resources and support, Mark did the rest.

Here was a boy who never before had found an outlet for his creativity. He had gone through school as an underachiever who read the assignments, filled in the worksheets, and performed when required to do so—but always marginally, because he was uninspired. He slopped though such assignments with a C average, just enough to keep the teacher and parents off his neck.

If I were to create a profile for Mark, these are some of the descriptions I'd use:

- works creatively
- tinkers
- understands that failing is part of inventive process
- loves to talk about ideas
- loves to find solutions
- operates all senses
- learns three-dimensionally
- thrives on choices
- is artistic
- shows mechanical talent
- is intrinsically motivated
- likes ambiguity
- likes to share expertise
- exhibits high energy when allowed to create
- is messy until finished
- is visually astute
- learns more through observation than through reading
- can't tolerate worksheets

Often, these traits are not valued and encouraged in learners.

Many kids, from my experience, have this kind of learning style, and the creating classroom is made to order for them. This environment permits them to realize their own powers, perhaps for the first time, and to develop a new sense of self. Often they are amazed at the status they have gained in the eyes of their classmates. In turn, they become made-to-order resources for their classmates, who don't hesitate to come to them for help.

Mark's story is one of those happy stories. I believe that students like Mark abound in our classrooms and need to be given an outlet for their creativity.

Brenda's Story

Brenda was mainstreamed into my classroom from a special education class. Coming from a very prescriptive environment, she stepped into a whirl of activity via project learning—a drastic change for Brenda. Would it work? We wondered, and then we tried it!

At first Brenda, quite stubborn and opinionated, just stood back and watched. Soon, however, she wanted the same kind of attention and feedback the other students received because they were actively involved. Because Brenda was not as independent as other students, it was necessary to invest extra time and support in getting her involved. This came in the form of Mrs. Harris, a very understanding and dedicated volunteer. In addition, Brenda's classmates often went out of their way to help her.

Thus Brenda became part of our community of learners as we set about to create that year's version of Washington, DC. Though she sometimes got frustrated and angry (and pouty), Brenda joined in with our making and doing and learning, expressing her opinion loudly and freely. It was her right to do so. Learning is for everyone. And Brenda did learn.

By luck of the draw, Brenda's building was the Museum of Natural History. Mrs. Harris helped Brenda find pictures of the building, read about it, and decide what to include inside the museum. Then she worked with Brenda to design and construct it. Brenda's way of learning was slower than some of her classmates', with lots of restarts and talking through steps. But Brenda made her own choices about what to include, assembled her own materials, and constructed her own building. On Tour Day, she conducted tours and experienced the exhilaration of working and completing a project along with her classmates.

It is important to note that students such as Brenda must be expected to do their own work, but need a lot of support. When you ask a volunteer to work with a student like Brenda, it is important to be sure that the person has the patience and temperament to guide and assist the student without doing the actual work. The project may turn out to be beautiful, or it may not, but it must be the student's own work, just as it is with every other student.

Community Spirit

So far we have met Keith, Gerald, Mark, and Brenda, each with a very different personality and different ways of learning and thinking. A powerful advantage of the creating classroom is that it capitalizes on the strengths of all learners. Students learn from one another as they observe how classmates figure out how to solve problems. Furthermore, no one has to compete, because all are involved in diverse activities. How can the zoo compete with the National Archives? Yet everyone feels able to contribute to the community effort.

This community spirit is heartwarming. Students help each other, experiment together, and root for one another. Learning is not an isolated activity. We come to understand that no one knows everything, that others know things we don't. Often what we don't know is the very thing that someone else does know and will share with us. This is an important lesson of life.

Most children learn to accommodate other children, even those with poor social skills or learning problems. Some become self-appointed helpers, some are watchful but cautious, and some avoid the situation altogether. A few are confrontational; another problem that has to be solved.

The creating classroom cannot function without cooperation and the mutual respect of everyone—students, teacher, and volunteers. One thing that I insisted on at all times was that the students be kind to and show respect for one another. In turn, I tried to model that respectful behavior and expected the other students to follow my example. When someone didn't, I talked privately with that person.

Sarah's Story

Sarah was in the Gifted and Talented program in the school, but she still had important lessons to learn during the Washington, DC, project. Aloof by nature, Sarah tended to stand apart from her classmates.

Sarah's talents were academic and artistic. For her part of Washington, DC, she constructed the U.S. Supreme Court building. For background she reviewed over fifty Supreme Court cases and read several biographies of Supreme Court justices. After a careful study of the architecture of the Supreme Court building, she made a detailed replica, inside and out, with beautiful columns, artwork, and other details. When you lifted the roof, you would see a wonderful miniature version of the interior of the building. There were the nine justices of the Supreme Court, and Sandra Day O'Connor was unmistakable. Sarah truly became an expert on the judicial branch of our government, and experienced the joy of pursuing an interest in depth and combining her many talents to work toward a goal.

Sarah's classmates respected her talents and skills but were not satisfied to let her get by without sharing them. Somehow they prevailed, and her aloofness was forgotten. Much to her own amazement, she found herself talking and sharing extensively. No longer an isolated creator, she joined into the community spirit and collaborated with many classmates on how to build this or that, or what to pursue for research. Also to her surprise, she found that she learned much by communicating with everyone in class.

Sarah could go as far as her talents and energy could take her, and that was far. Because projects like Washington, DC, and Latin America are very open ended, they provide unlimited learning environments for students like Sarah, who need to be stretched and awakened to their potential. Such projects also enable them to become teachers, in a sense, by helping and instructing classmates. They come to realize the truth in the saying that we learn best when we teach others.

Jan's Story

Jan was a capable student who needed cajoling and prodding to finish anything. She didn't take responsibility and she didn't take risks. Here was Jan facing construction of the Amazon River Basin with all its accoutrements, flora, and fauna, and she couldn't get started. The Amazon, with its various and unique parts, is a rather far-reaching assignment, and one that had to be completed, or there would certainly be an enormous empty space in South America.

Jan would half-heartedly try something and discard it, or just sit and stare at the space on the floor. She was afraid to take the risk of placing herself on the map. For many of us, exposing our own work to the world can be a frightening experience because we are afraid of being criticized or embarrassed. However, we must help students understand that an important aspect of learning is making mistakes and learning from them. It is a new idea for many students.

Jan's first task was overcoming inertia. She had hidden behind safe answers and a fill-in-the-blank mentality for years. So we started on one small task, a tree for the Amazon—messed around with it, talked about various ways to make a tree, redid it several times, and finally ended up with something that looked very much like a miniature tree. I assisted Jan through this first process so that she could see how to learn through making mistakes—and to get comfortable with that idea. After that, she hesitantly began another tree on her own, and I supported her. Then she switched to making animals and then to the Amazon. Each time Jan took on a new task, it was easier, and she gained confidence. Step by step she was weaned from needing constant adult affirmation.

Students like Jan need support and encouragement to escape from reliance on the teacher as the source of all information. Actually the Amazon soon flourished under Jan's care, and she even found humor in those first wobbly trees and plants.

Alex's Story

Alex had to take care of himself, because no one else did. Our classroom project provided him with a sense of purpose and belonging that had been missing from his life. Alex possessed excellent organizational skills, and took it upon himself to keep the rest of us organized. At first, classmates were nonplussed at Alex's industrious housekeeping, but they soon began to rely on him. In turn, their friendliness and warm regard toward Alex provided him with the affirmation he was missing at home.

One morning at the very beginning of the Washington, DC, project, I came into the classroom and was overwhelmed by a huge pile of cardboard boxes of various sizes and shapes heaped in the middle of the room. As I surveyed the scene, Alex popped out of a large carton and yelled, "Surprise!" He had spent hours scrounging these boxes from stores and alleys so that students could use them for their projects. He had made many trips on foot carrying and dragging them to school.

I could not possibly discourage such industry and dedication. When this kind of enthusiasm and excitement occurs, we must capture it! As the other students gathered that morning, we rearranged the desks to accommodate the unexpected contribution, and sat for a while wondering what the boxes would become. It was quite an experience to ponder a pile of boxes and envision a wonderful city. Someone took pictures of the pile, and later we compared it to our completed city.

This event marked the beginning of Alex's helpfulness. From time to time, he replenished our supply of cardboard. For once in his life, he found that he was an important part of a close-knit group—and he thrived on the experience. As the cardboard pile was transformed into various buildings, Alex continued to keep us organized.

Of course, Alex had his own project to build, the Library of Congress. Still, he found time periodically to check the Washington, DC, map to make sure things were being put in their proper places—buildings, bridges, the Potomac River, cherry trees, and escaped zoo animals. After school, he would delight in taking everything off the map, sweeping it clean, and then replacing everything just so. Alex's classmates were delighted, too. Students like Sarah, Keith, Gerald, Brenda, and many others were not organizers, and they relied on Alex's help.

Alex put his talents to good use for Tour Day. He prepared the invitation to parents and set up a list of who would bring cookies, punch, napkins, and a bouquet for the refreshment table. Though his parents were "too busy" to come for a tour, Alex managed to hide his hurt by keeping active and helping others. A highlight for Alex came when he gave two impressive tours to other visitors.

Perhaps no one took care of Alex, but Alex certainly took care of us.

5

A Philosophy of Creating

The Supreme Court [Building], which consisted of Betty Crocker cake mix, homemade icing, one-half of a hamburger bun, several uncooked spaghetti sticks, a couple wads of chewed gum, and two Hershey chocolate bars, will always be a great memory for me. This was the first project that allowed me to explore my own abilities and take pride in a creation being completed by myself. I remember being very excited during the "tour" of Washington, DC, and feeling very satisfied with my work.

— John Schwoebel, former student

*T*he only real adventure in learning is *creating.* Notice that I did not say *creativity,* which is an overworked and often misunderstood term. Creating absorbs the student in assimilating the external world into his or her own internal world. Creating involves the processes of assembling ideas into personal meaning. No one is too young to experience the joy of creating.

Creating may be found in many forms. Problem solving, experimenting, building, writing, hypothesizing, planning, organizing, and adapting are examples of activities experienced by students who are creating. The key to creating—adventures in learning and active minds—is classroom environment. We must offer an environment where such activities are not only permitted, but actively encouraged. We must provide experiences for students to investigate, analyze, and problem solve; in short, we must stimulate higher levels of thinking in our students. We haven't been looking at activities for busy work or cute crafts (eyewash), but at a real effort to push each student to the limits of his or her thinking potential.

Attitudes and Tolerance

How does one develop a classroom environment for creating? Such an environment requires flexible attitudes on the part of teacher and students. As the teacher you must ask yourself, "Do I really believe that children should be engaged in higher order thinking skills?" If your answer is yes, you have more questions to consider. "Am I flexible enough to enjoy establishing a creating classroom?" "Can I live with ambiguity and a messy classroom?" "Do I want to look at accountability from new perspectives?" If the answers are still yes, you are reading this book as it is intended to be read.

What about your students? This will be a change for them also. They will have to become more active in their learning, which can be a jolt until they catch on. A number of students may find it difficult to adapt to this change if they are used to being spoon-fed. It is easier to follow instructions blindly than it is to be an active participant. I must admit to feeling that way myself at times: "Just tell me what to do!" However, from personal experience and from observing students, I know that the active choice is the only one with staying power. Easy answers undermine the development of thinking skills.

Creating *Creating:* Setting Up Your Classroom

Let us examine several ideas that support and promote a creating classroom.

Fiddling—the essence of creating   Students need the opportunity to fiddle with pieces of their world, which consists of physical things and mental things—observations, words, thoughts, ideas, gadgets, trinkets, books, pictures, curiosity, unresolved mysteries. Some people, both parents and teachers, see a child's fiddling as trivial or irritating, something to ignore or to correct. However, it is a natural behavior of human beings. People acquire a large part of their knowledge and understanding through fiddling with things and ideas. So it is with our students.

Fiddling produces juxtapositions that can stimulate new insights when strange or unusual images and/or ideas appear together. To promote productive fiddling in the classroom, we must supply useful raw materials, both mental and physical. As a teacher, I like to assemble physical tools such as glue guns, cardboard, magazines, books, pictures, models, art supplies, and lots more. To guide the use of the physical tools, we must provide appropriate mental raw materials—ideas, conversations, questions, patterns, facts, images, problems—bits and pieces needed to make mental connections and mental pictures.

In my experience, once students understand the concept of fiddling, they generate much of their own physical and mental raw materials for their projects. As they do so, their conversations change from trivial and begin to focus on what they are doing, thinking, and creating. These are giant steps toward becoming independent and autonomous learners.

Mental raw materials

There is much talk in educational circles today about promoting higher-level thinking: critical thinking, creativity, and problem solving. Unfortunately, much of the discussion is misinformed. Too many people assume that a student can simply be a critical thinker or simply be creative without attention to building an adequate foundation for these higher-order mental activities. It is essential for teachers to understand that students cannot think critically or create without a solid base of information—facts, details, and understandings.

The teaching and learning of facts and details are much maligned these days. In truth, facts, details, and understandings are the tools with which we all think. By manipulating them, we develop concepts, generalizations, products, and solutions. It is essential, therefore, to teach facts, details, and understandings either before or in conjunction with high-level activities.

The jigsaw puzzle—a metaphor about details

Imagine that someone gave you a five-hundred-piece jigsaw puzzle for your birthday. Imagine that it came in a plain brown box with no picture of the puzzle on the outside. No big picture! No details to study to arrive at the big picture! You are expected to assemble five hundred pieces into a picture that you know nothing about and can't even begin to guess at.

This is a metaphor for attempting to teach higher-level thinking skills without providing the students with any of the facts and details required for the final product. For example, if students are assigned to make some classroom rules that do not violate the Bill of Rights, they need to know the "big picture" and all the "pieces" of the Bill of Rights. Without understanding the facts and details, the students will rely on guess, personal preference, and hearsay, and come up with a worthless product, and will have wasted a lot of time on a worthless exercise.

A graphic example would be the construction of a building for the Washington, DC, project. How can anyone build a model of the White House without ever having seen a picture or model, or the building itself? Obviously the details of the building are important to someone constructing a model of it.

Understanding the levels of thinking and learning

One way to understand terms such as *higher-level thinking, critical thinking, creativity,* and *problem solving* is to see how they relate to Bloom's *Taxonomy of Educational Objectives: Cognitive Domain.* Bloom's *Taxonomy* provides an important framework for understanding the full range of thinking processes. Bloom identifies six levels of thinking arranged in a hierarchy with knowledge as the lowest, although the other five levels utilize knowledge in various ways. Below is a brief introduction to Bloom's *Taxonomy,* followed by answers to the question, "What is higher-level thinking?"

Level 1: *Knowledge.* The knowledge level involves the learning of facts or factual information, but is limited to recognizing or remembering that information at a later time. This requires memorizing. While this is low-level thinking, it is an essential step toward higher-level thinking. It is impossible, for example, to design a model of the Washington Monument without knowing some facts about it. Likewise, it is necessary for students to know and remember the functions of the three branches of government before they can analyze them, which requires higher-level thinking.

Level 2: *Comprehension.* Comprehension involves using facts in a limited way, such as a student's using his or her own words to describe the Lincoln Memorial, or to explain how a bill becomes a law. By contrast, a student who merely recites a textbook definition of the U.S. Constitution is thinking only at the knowledge level.

Level 3: *Application.* Application involves using factual information in a new context. Building Ford's Theater *to scale* requires the application of math and measurement skills. Writing letters to U.S. Senators and Representatives requires the application of *writing skills,* not to mention those of penmanship, formatting a letter, and addressing an envelope properly. On the other hand, the *composition* of a letter is synthesis, which is level five.

Level 4: *Analysis.* Analysis requires the learner to distinguish details and the relationships among them. Transforming a picture of the Petersen House to a recognizable model requires a lot of analysis, as well as application. Likewise, analysis is involved when students understand the cause-and-effect relationships of the Bill of Rights to their personal lives.

Level 5: *Synthesis.* Synthesis requires the creation of a new product. The student's finished project is a synthesis, as are historical fiction and original artwork done for the project. The students are involved in written and oral synthesis activities when preparing for Tour Day.

Level 6: *Evaluation.* Evaluation requires judgement on the part of the students, but it goes beyond their opinions. Opinions are generally based on emotion or incomplete information, whereas evaluation is based on information and specific criteria. Choosing the best or most appropriate materials for constructing the students' buildings requires evaluation. So does choosing the most appropriate details to include in their Tour Day presentations.

So, what is higher-level thinking? Higher-level thinking includes Bloom's levels three through six: critical thinking is evaluation, and creativity and creative thinking require synthesis. Problem solving can be application if the answer is convergent (predetermined), or it can be synthesis if the answer is divergent (open-ended). When you try to decide which level a thinking task may be, remember that each level includes all those before it. Thus you place it at the highest possible level.

Be assured that the creating classroom challenges students to work at all six of Bloom's levels of thinking and learning.

Creating Takes Time

The way students learn is heavily influenced by the use of time. Since there is a lot to accomplish each day in a classroom, we don't dare abuse time. I decided what I needed to do was to invent more time. The following sections describe the steps I took.

Analyzing lessons First, I looked at what was happening during various lessons that I taught. I noted that each lesson has three phases: a beginning phase, a middle phase, and an ending phase. Not too profound, I know. However, I analyzed what takes place during each segment of time. The beginning phase requires start-up time. We get our stuff (pencils, books, paper, or whatever), settle ourselves in our spots, try to free our minds from the previous lesson, and get ready to concentrate on the new task. The start of a new lesson is a time of low productivity.

Then we move into the middle phase, the heart of the lesson, where productive activity is taking place. Students are involved in their work, whether it is mental, physical, or both. They are concentrating and thinking. But soon that passes, and we approach the end of the lesson. I also noticed that students past the half-way mark of the middle phase begin watching the clock to see how long until the end of the lesson. This, of course, is a distraction. Furthermore, the end of a lesson does not include a lot of productivity, but more a gathering (or dropping) of materials, thinking ahead to recess, and what-have-you.

As I analyzed these lessons, I decided that I must make the middle portion much longer so that more productivity could take place. This means dividing the time available into longer periods, but fewer of them. With fewer divisions, you have fewer beginning and ending phases. Of course, this means restructuring your daily schedule.

I can assure you that students do have long attention spans and can work for extended periods of time if they are involved in a meaningful activity. I believe that is a strength of project teaching (or whole learning)—students discover the pleasure of extended times of thinking and doing. By making the middle of a lesson much longer, you are using time more wisely. Instead of choppy lessons throughout the day, you gain productive time by reducing the number of beginning and ending phases.

Integrating skills and content
Another way to invent time is to integrate the teaching of two or more subjects. A social studies project lends itself easily and naturally to the incorporation of reading, language arts, math, science, and art. While students are researching social studies content, they will be reading and writing, sketching or drawing, and measuring and calculating, as well as manipulating ideas and materials. Thus you are getting much more mileage (learning) for the time invested.

The students are also integrating their personal skills and talents. In our world, it is a must for people to be able to combine multiple skills and talents for specific tasks, both at home and in the work place. A classroom project likewise requires students to combine their academic and personal skills to accomplish their tasks. This is a wise and efficient use of time. Why should students practice math skills only during math class? Why should students write compositions only during language arts period or use art skills only during art period? Once a learner experiences the opportunity to bring multiple skills and talents on a specific task, he or she has entered the real world, because that is the way the real world works. Such opportunities also bring pleasure and joy to their learning.

Using time wisely
If we are inventing time, we must use it wisely; purposeful time is our goal. Nothing is worse than a classroom filled with students horsing around and not using their time productively. In the midst of chaos or a free-for-all mentality, students cannot concentrate on their tasks. You, the teacher, must structure the day so that students are truly working. They must concentrate energy upon their project, and it is up to you to orchestrate that energy. There is a time for productive noise when students are building, using glue guns, and brushing paint—fully engaged in an active environment. On the other hand, there will be times when a quiet classroom is needed for students to engage in the quiet mental activity involved in acquiring information and working with the higher-order thinking skills.

Blessed solitude   Quite accidentally one day we had a morning of solitude. Each student was alone in his or her private world of thinking and doing. The work had progressed to a point where every student had loose ends—ideas and tasks—to pursue. I suggested that we spend a half-hour in silence while they worked on their tasks. They were free to move around while they worked on their projects, but there was to be no talking. I loved it, and amazingly, so did the kids! By the end of the half-hour, they asked if we could spend the whole morning that way. So we did. The students found great satisfaction concentrating on what they were mentally and physically collecting.

They wrote, built, read, and contemplated in silence. They made the rule and I enforced it—no talking—and it worked. So from that day on, and in succeeding years, we had solitude mornings. Many students have commented afterward that those solitude mornings were the first time they understood how learning takes place.

Cut Out the Nonsense

Probably I should couch this in educational jargon; however, this is what I want to say—I cut out a lot of the nonsense from my curriculum. We didn't have popcorn parties, movies every week (that many students had already seen), or anything else of that ilk. I tried to make time work for us. Once students get involved in this kind of learning environment, they are hooked, and they never did whine for popcorn or movies.

Collaboration: Student Interaction and Communication

Project work requires collaboration. Collaboration in the classroom means close interaction, communication, and sharing among students, teachers, principal, and volunteers. How do all these people collaborate in a creating classroom?

If your classroom is based on the philosophy that all people have different talents and skills and that sharing these talents and skills enriches everyone, it isn't difficult. There will be both an informal and a formal sharing. Each of the following is a way of collaborating. As the teacher, you provide the framework for appropriate formal and informal collaboration.

Discussions and conversations
Students love to discuss their work. My students found it quite an exhilarating experience to converse about history, government, architecture, construction, and a variety of other topics related to the project. During the project, the entire class quite often would become involved in discussions. I might start the discussion rolling with some questions, or often times a student would start the discussion with a question of his or her own.

These discussions were an excellent way to make important connections among the many things being learned. In this way the students, having already acquired knowledge and comprehension (the lower levels of Bloom's taxonomy), could discuss these topics at the higher levels. This gave them the opportunity to use the new vocabulary they were acquiring and to test their ideas against other students. There was quite a difference in the level of discussions as the project progressed; students began discussing ideas, points of view, and interpretations from a basis of knowledge rather than opinion. Everyone had contributions to make to these discussions.

Of course, conversations took place, too. I suppose this is a fancy word for talking. While the discussions involved the whole class, the conversations were informal and took place among various students at various times. I must admit that sometimes when I saw students talking, I would rush over to give them my general disapproval and to get them on task, only to find that they were talking about the things I wanted them to. Surprise! They might be talking about the ideas of Abraham Lincoln, or about how to use a glue gun. The students were truly enjoying learning.

Sharing new insights
Students discover new insights in a creating classroom and experience that wonderful "aha" feeling. This is a new experience for many of them, and the excitement should be shared. You, the teacher, must value this excitement and be excited also. The classroom is the place where ideas should flow. Sharing is a powerful motivator for many students.

Kids teaching classmates

Teaching equals learning. No doubt you have heard the old teaching cliche, "I never really understood it until I had to teach it." As teachers, we know that this is often true; if we have taught something, it stays with us, while just reading about something or memorizing it doesn't guarantee mental staying power. Teaching someone else engages us in the material and provides us with a purpose for learning it.

Why shouldn't our students have the same experience? My students did. During their conversations and discussions, students found themselves teaching their classmates. Likewise, on Tour Day, the students found themselves teaching our guests about Washington, DC, or Latin America.

Questioning: Autonomy and collaboration

A sage once said that learning is what happens when we find answers to questions. If the sage knew what he (or she) was talking about, it follows that students should be asking questions—lots of them. The trouble with many students is that when they ask questions, they expect the teacher to give all the answers and solutions. Worse yet, many teachers think that they are supposed to give all the answers. Thus the students are given no responsibility for their own learning, and they remain dependent learners rather than becoming independent learners.

Students need to be taught to ask meaningful questions, then be taught to find some of the answers or solutions themselves. In the real world, answers and solutions are not always easy to find, and the classroom should reflect this reality. This is not to say that the teacher never answers a question, but rather the teacher works with the students to help them develop some autonomy in their learning.

In a creating classroom, students should be asking lots of questions, addressed to themselves individually and addressed to the group. This is a step toward personal autonomy. And what about the questions that have more than one answer, or those with no solution at all? An autonomous learner will keep questing to discover answers and solutions.

If a lot of questions are being asked, there will be collaboration among the people in your classroom. Besides autonomy, students need to learn that it is all right to collaborate in their quest for information.

It becomes natural to discuss ideas and to question other people about what they know or think. The wonderful thing is that with so many students using all of their talents and strengths, there are many sources for solutions.

Once students begin asking questions and testing hypotheses and solutions, they can't rest until they find one that satisfies them. This intellectual tension is invaluable for learning. It may lead students to progress to higher levels of thinking and to the manipulation of their ideas. They begin to question beyond the first question: the first answer leads to another question that needs a solution, and then another and another. Thus students learn another way to push to their limits of thinking, problem solving, and creating.

Brainstorming   Brainstorming is a great way to start ideas flowing. This is a somewhat structured technique for generating ideas and promoting creativity. In the elementary classroom, the teacher will be the group leader who poses a question that requires a solution. The group members (the class) respond with as many ideas as they can think of. Because it is a group process, many ideas come forth, and new ideas often spring from someone hearing someone else's idea. This is called *hitchhiking* an idea.

Often students need ideas for their projects. One such question I have used to promote brainstorming is, "How can we design cherry trees for the Potomac?" You would be amazed at how many ideas a class can think of to make cherry trees!

Because brainstorming is a group process, certain rules are necessary to make it work:

1. No one is permitted to criticize any idea. The ideas will be evaluated at a later stage.
2. Wild ideas are welcome and encouraged. With a little tinkering, wild ideas often become useful.
3. The group should generate as many ideas as possible. The more ideas to choose from, the better the chance of finding some good ones.
4. The ideas already generated may be improved or combined. Hitchhiking on someone else's idea often produces a better idea.

A key feature of the process is that no one is allowed to criticize another student's idea, thus they may generate many ideas without the fear of being ridiculed. Students should be encouraged to produce many random possibilities, think of outrageous ideas—the wilder the better. Later, they'll sort through the ideas to try to find a solution, but the ideas must not be judged at the time they are offered. In the world of inventions, many true innovations were the result of ideas that at first seemed too farfetched to be considered. Ideas will be generated only if closure has not taken place; premature closure (selecting ideas too soon) will shut down the process.

Providing Appropriate Feedback

Students need feedback if they are going to improve. If you have an atmosphere where students are creating, asking questions, making mistakes and learning from them, and looking for solutions, then feedback is a vital element of learning.

Feedback should be used for encouragement and support, as well as for assistance and correction. Appropriate feedback should be in the form of metacognition. The teacher needs to help students think out loud about the processes they are working with (such as how to make the dome for the Capitol). The teacher should start a dialogue about several solutions that are available for solving the problem.

A student once came to me with a problem he was having with designing the columns of the Jefferson Memorial. Actually they looked pretty good. However, he wanted to learn more by going beyond what he had already done. He said, "Don't be a mom and just tell me it looks great. Help me so I can get better and be an architect someday." I learned a lot that day. How often do we slide quickly over something if it looks satisfactory, and not help the student discover new ideas or possibilities? And how often do we automatically give praise and neglect to help students accomplish more?

Feedback from other students is most valuable. Often students care more about what peers think than what adults think. Students tend to be honest in their criticism, even if they lack tact at times. Furthermore, peer feedback helps the student who gives it as well as the student who receives it. In a creating classroom, this is another valuable form of collaboration.

Wanted: Flexible Minds

Teachers must assure students that it is all right for them to change their minds. If students are in an experimental phase of work, or looking for tentative solutions, it is very likely that results, plans, or ideas will change. This comes as a surprise to many students, and it takes time for them to assimilate the idea. Students need to be able to start a building, decide it isn't what they envisioned, and start over or make adjustments. Similarly, they need to be able to write a story about their project and then decide to rewrite it. Discarding part of their work will make many students uncomfortable. They generally assume that once something is under way, that's it. For many, the concepts of rethinking, redesigning, tearing apart, adjusting, or starting over have never entered their minds. In a creating classroom, we must make sure that the idea of suspending judgment and keeping an open mind with the option of changing one's direction becomes part of their thinking.

In the process of thinking and doing, we all make mistakes. It is important to learn from those mistakes, and make the process a positive experience. Unfortunately, we are nervous with this concept in our classrooms. As teachers, we often program our students for the quick right answer and penalize them if they are wrong. When they correct a mistake, it is with a sense of desperation and relief, with little reflective thought and only to meet teacher expectations. It may take time for both the students and the teacher to accept making mistakes as a positive step toward learning, but expecting instant correctness is the antithesis of a creating classroom.

How do we overcome the students' fear of making mistakes? First, it is important that we do not penalize students for taking risks and making mistakes, or else students will always fear making them and won't learn from them. It is also important to slow down the pace of the classroom. Give students time to reflect on, analyze, and evaluate what they are doing, change their minds, and learn from their mistakes. Action and contemplation need to be balanced.

If a student has to race from one superficial lesson to the next, how can he or she learn to think, contemplate, learn from trial and error, or change ideas or products? As teachers, we have designed too many response lessons where the deadline must be met, rather than building an environment for flexible minds.

Three-dimensional thinking

Life is a three-dimensional experience, but too often school is not. We live in a 3-D world powered by 3-D thinking. Too often schools only offer students 1-D and 2-D experiences. Experiences requiring fill-in-the-blank worksheets, true-false answers, rote learning, recitation of facts, and round-robin reading sessions are examples of 1-D and 2-D activities. These will not produce much of the learning (or thinking) that is required for living in a 3-D world.

What is three-dimensional thinking? It is participating in one's education by assimilating and processing images, thoughts, ideas, and physical phenomena. It requires the active manipulation of our physical and mental environments in a thoughtful and meaningful way. It involves the higher levels of Bloom's taxonomy.

Too often, people think of three-dimensional as referring only to physical things. In the Washington, DC, project, there was always the danger that people would see only the physical aspects, not recognizing the mental environment that lay just beneath the surface. One could not exist without the other.

Using the physical world to enhance thinking can help students develop a more sophisticated understanding of how their world is arranged. Learners become more aware of the relevance of details and their relationships—organizational patterns, cause and effect, spatial relationships, comparisons, analogies, and so on. The creating classroom often uses the physical environment as a source of knowledge and ideas that the students will process through 3-D thinking. The physical environment provides context, meaning, and relevance for information encountered by the student.

The teacher must help students bridge the gap between the physical and mental environments by providing physical materials and mental tasks to be performed. For example, measuring, calculating, mapping, researching, writing, constructing, communicating, performing an experiment, conducting a survey, drawing, and painting are a few ways of bridging this gap.

Humor

Humor is essential for an intellectually creative classroom. I once had a student teacher who was having trouble managing the class. She asked me what some of my most useful techniques were. When I said using humor was a great technique for smoothing problems, she replied that she couldn't see anything funny in a classroom. And she didn't. But I did, and I feel humor is an essential management tool for any classroom. Laughter, smiles, and chuckles make life in a classroom happier and more pleasant. These are important ingredients in a creating classroom.

When we learn through mistakes and trial and error, funny things will occur along the way. Better to see the positive humor, laugh, and go on, than to insult or humiliate a student who has made a mistake. If a student feels humiliated because of a mistake, not much learning from mistakes will take place in that classroom. Instead, the classroom will become a place where there is one right answer and students only respond if they know it.

If you want a creating classroom, you and the students must be accepting of new and unusual ideas that elicit a positive chuckle or laugh rather than a negative reaction.

For example, one of my students was making the Washington Monument, so he very excitedly hauled in a large refrigerator box. The box—which he intended to use in its entirety—was at least five times too big. The opportunity was ripe for derision and ridicule, but here was a student who made a lot of effort to secure this huge box, get it to school, and show excitement for his project. These are very positive attributes. Realistically though, it was just too big. We looked at the box's size and the size of the map and room, discussed pros and cons, and laughed. Since the atmosphere was one of creating and learning from mistakes, the situation was handled good naturedly.

There are times when feelings get hurt in any classroom. When or if it happens, teachers and students need to apologize. This in itself is another learning experience on acceptance.

In Conclusion

You have meandered through my philosophy on creating. It is a philosophy based on experiences—mine and those of many students. Early in my teaching life, I discovered that teaching can be boring and ineffective. Fortunately, I asked myself some questions about what was going on in my classroom, and found some solutions to those answers. This changed my life and the lives of my students—all for the better.

The questions I asked were rather simple, and so were the answers. Solutions were more difficult. What do I want my students to achieve? Are we using our time wisely? Are my students experiencing the pleasures of learning? I have continued to ask questions such as these throughout my teaching life. This is an endeavor that must continue as long as we work with students of any age—the asking of questions and the seeking and testing of solutions.

6

Reflections and Flashbacks: Things I Have Learned

We look at the present through a rear-view mirror. We march backwards into the future.

— Marshall McLuhan, *The Medium Is the Massage*

Today's television child is attuned to up-to-the-minute "adult" news—inflation, rioting, war, taxes, crime, bathing beauties— and is bewildered when he enters the nineteenth-century environ- ment that still characterizes the educational establishment where information is scarce but ordered and structured by fragmented, classified patterns, subjects, and schedules. It is naturally an environment much like any factory set-up with its inventories and assembly lines.

— Marshall McLuhan, *The Medium Is the Massage*

About Looking Back

Writing this book has forced me to examine how I teach and what I think. As I have rummaged around in my mind, I have discovered many ideas that were valuable to me in my growth as a teacher. Just as students learn by observing and acting on their observations, so do teachers. We must take time to think and ask why we are doing what we are doing. Sometimes the answer is disturbing. The following is a collection of bits and pieces of wisdom I've gleaned over the years.

About Collecting Stuff

One day it occurred to me that I wasn't using all the stuff I had spent years collecting for my classroom. I had filled my basement with the overflow. There came to be piles of outdated bulletin board materials, workbooks, brochures, pamphlets, advertising materials, old ditto sheets, plastic gizmos, and magazines by the ton. They were just gathering dust and getting in my way. Why wasn't I using them? Because they weren't things appropriate for project-centered teaching.

I had changed my style of teaching, and now the students created their own bulletin board materials, wrote assignments from scratch, and were involved in projects. And each year was a fresh beginning for a new group of students. They did their own thinking, building, and creating, and made their own meaning. They were building their own minds, not trying to imitate someone else's.

I threw all that stuff out of my basement. Now I have a great reading room down there. Marshall McLuhan was right about many things.

About Worksheets

If we truly believe that minds develop by making meaning from experience, then how can we thrust one worksheet after another upon our students? Real learning is about messing around with ideas, reflecting on our actions, learning through mistakes, making connections about the world, and brainstorming with a community of learners.

Too many classrooms are based on the McLuhanesque factory model, where each subject is discrete and students move through as if on an assembly line, each being filled with "stuff" as he or she moves by. Each subject is allotted a certain number of minutes, and each student is exposed to only that much. Subject matter, outcomes, skills, and facts are predetermined and simple to test and to account for.

This model requires a lot of "stuffing," and much of it is produced by the copy machine. It is passionless, connectionless, difficult to motivate, and it produces low-quality learning. Students memorize the "stuffing" in order to pass a test, then forget it. Reports from the trenches indicate that not only do students occasionally fall asleep, but more than one teacher has done likewise.

For many teachers, not using worksheets may seem like an extreme position. I'll concede that a few worksheets might be acceptable—but only under certain conditions. First, they must be made for your classroom by you or the students or both. Second, they must be made to fit the project that you are working on at that particular time. This eliminates all packaged generic worksheets that supposedly fit every classroom in America.

While I am criticizing factory-model schools, we might look at another parallel between the factory and some classrooms—escape from monotony. Factories use work breaks to make life in the factory more tolerable. Some classrooms use "free time" and parties to make life in the classroom more tolerable. In the case of the classroom, this is an admission that classroom work is unpleasant and that escape is a treat. Is this really how we want students to feel about school work? School assignments should carry their own rewards—the joy of learning and the pleasure of using minds.

I'll admit that I wanted to escape from worksheets when I was a young student, but who wouldn't? On the other hand, you have to chase students out of the classroom at noon and after school when a good project is underway. Students deserve more than worksheets, and I believe that the world demands more. The needs of tomorrow are so great and diversified that worksheets cannot adequately prepare students for anything important.

About the Future

As teachers, we must think about the future. I found myself concentrating too narrowly on my work at home and school, and when I came up for air, I was amazed that so many other things were happening and changing. Some of the changes in our world intrude themselves into our classrooms, and others need to be acknowledged and introduced. Students are certainly aware of changes. As teachers, we can't produce the same classroom year after year, for if we do, we will slip into irrelevance. Instead, we must keep our classroom viable and vital and full of fresh air.

In order to expand our vision of teaching and learning, we need to look at the world. Teachers must be aware of what is happening and in what direction it appears to be going. The world we know today is likely to have disappeared within twenty-five years, and our students must be provided with powerful skills for the world of tomorrow—skills in comprehending, thinking, learning, writing, and adapting to change.

Therefore, we need to keep an eye on the future when we plan today's lessons. Which of today's vital issues will bring about tomorrow's changes? What do others predict for the future? If we don't know about the future, how can we prepare for today? Tomorrow? Next year? The future belongs to all of us, and as teachers we need to collaborate and help create it. We must brainstorm the future together.

About Parallel Lives

Most children live two separate, parallel lives: school and non-school. Too often, classroom life is separated from the child's other life. McLuhan, at the beginning of this chapter, presents an extreme view of these separate lives. He goes on to say, "Today's child is growing up absurd, because he lives in two worlds, and neither of them inclines him to grow up. Growing up—that is our new work, and it is *total*. Mere instruction will not suffice" (18).

This division does not, however, advocate the cliche of "the classroom versus the real world." The classroom is an important part of the world and of the life of the child—but is often too far removed from the rest. Children become aware of this division in their lives.

The classroom serves a unique function in the life of a child, but we must not make it too remote from his or her other experiences. In the larger world, children do watch and listen to other people, and they do memorize things, and they also do many other things besides. In the classroom, we need to emulate the normal patterns and activities of children. Classroom life must not be restricted to watching or listening to someone else, reading a dry book, or doing the same kind of memorizing day after day. Classroom life must include delving, exploring, discovering, and understanding—learning in depth.

A truly educated person is one who has acquired a wide range of experiences, knowledge, skills, and perceptions. For this person, the world is broad, and life is physical and emotional, as well as intellectual.

This is how children should be growing up—integrating the separate parts of their lives into a single whole—making schooling an integral part of their lives.

About Asking Questions

Teachers need to ask questions about education—lots of them. Teachers should be excellent sources of good questions, since they watch education while it happens. I don't think we as teachers ask questions loudly enough, and often we don't know whom to ask. We should not be afraid to ask difficult questions, or questions we don't know the answers to. Here are some important questions to ask:

1. Should education be entertainment?
2. Should we teach today's "electronic" student with more electronics at school (TV, videos), or should we see ourselves as the last bastion of print and oral interaction with learners?
3. Are today's "electronic" students "wired" differently than students of a few years ago?
4. What are we going to do about values and moral and ethical development?
5. What is the latest research on the brain, and why aren't we incorporating it into the classroom?
6. How much stuff do we have to cover? How fast? Why?
7. Who are the "they" who won't let us do something?
8. What is education, anyway?

Hard questions can be uncomfortable to discuss, but I believe that we must ask hard questions about education and teaching and learning, and we must do this together for now and the future.

About Constructing Meaning

When a student encounters new information, he or she connects it with past knowledge and experience. From this interaction of the new with the old, the student interprets the new and constructs personal meaning. This is the *constructivist* view of learning: each learner constructs his or her own personal meaning from new information, and the meaning will vary from learner to learner.

The constructivist view of learning explains why all the students in your classroom don't arrive "knowing" the same things. Further, it shows that your students will differ greatly, and that they will react differently to the curriculum, to your teaching, and to one another. (Isn't this a reflection of the way the world really works?) Last but not least, it shows that they all will leave your classroom knowing things, but not always knowing all the *same* things. Acceptance of these realities will create a healthy environment for both teacher and students.

Project teaching provides a rich and varied set of experiences for students to use in constructing new meanings. The richer the experiences, the more profound will be the meanings. With this in mind, reconsider the sparseness of the workbook, and the poverty of that experience. Packaged curricula and formulas don't provide the kind of learning environment that students need. We must create appropriate learning environments—a creating classroom, project teaching, integration, 3-D learning, learning by observing, learning through mistakes, and learning by doing.

About My Best Teaching

I love to teach because I love to feel connected to students—to their ideas, moods, thinking, and the surprises of becoming lost in our work together. I love the laughter and even the frustrations as we throw away the superficial and try to become ourselves. When I'm part of this generative action, I'm teaching at my best. This happens during project teaching because the ever present sensation of adventure and discovery gives us—the students and me—motivation and perseverance, purpose in what we are doing, and a link to the outside world. On the other hand, I'm at my worst when I'm dishing out someone else's agenda and am not linked with the process. I cannot help students connect ideas if I am not working to connect them myself. I must be personally involved.

Of course, this means I, like the students, had to read, think, make buildings, experiment with organization, communicate with lots of people, make mistakes, mess around with ideas—in short, experience integration—in order to orchestrate a classroom environment for project teaching. Instead of grading worksheets or making bulletin boards after school, I might be constructing a building myself, or locating materials and resources, or just thinking—in order to get a feel for all the aspects of the project. Not only did we experience all this freedom (and fun), but we also did follow the district curriculum guide for U.S. social studies (or Latin America); we just pursued it our own way through project teaching.

All of this had a wonderful side benefit—the teacher grew intellectually. Teaching to promote student thinking gives the teacher an opportunity to think along with the students rather than to get mired down with routines and formulas. As teachers, we deserve this kind of renewal and freedom to use our expertise and creativity.

About Making Personal Connections

Everyone needs a passion for something, or else life is pretty boring. My passions are reading and teaching—and what a terrific combination! And I love to engage in the joys and pleasures of random reading—often unplanned and with unimagined outcomes. Who knows what fiction or nonfiction book will add some really important ideas to my life and my ways of thinking?

I have a friend who occasionally gives me a new stack of books to read, books that she knows I would never choose for myself. She is right, of course, but these books often broaden my vision and help me see life from different perspectives. Everything I read is grist for my mental mill, and you can never have too much grist for yourself and for your students. You'll discover yourself using it at the most unexpected times and in the most unexpected ways.

It is important for us as teachers to keep our receptors open to everything around us—not only for new books, but for new thoughts from whatever source. In this way we keep learning. If we are attuned to fresh ideas, we never know when something interesting might appear. If our receptors are shut down, we are certain to miss something important—and worse, we begin to get narrow and "old." Collecting and generating ideas should be requirements for being a teacher. In fact, the longer we teach, the more ideas we should have.

I think a teacher needs to be a "snoop" in the best sense of the word—snooping in order to learn and to make personal connections.

Why not visit shops that you wouldn't ordinarily step into, or invite conversation with people outside your own sphere? How about a new hobby? I have a teacher friend who became very interested in antiques and finally became part-owner of an antique store. Now he spends weekends and summers developing his new interest. As a result, he travels to markets for antiques, meets people with different points of view, and, not coincidentally, develops some terrific history ideas for his students.

Let's face it: How can you make interesting connections with knowledge and ideas if you don't have a large unprogrammed pool of information from which to choose? How can you possibly help students make connections if you don't? How can you help students with possibilities and adventures in learning if you don't have dozens of leads for them to explore and discover? If a book gives you only one good idea, or a new slant or something you've never thought of, or something that irritates you and makes you start to think, you have indeed stumbled on a great find. Even other people with irritating ideas can be a source of fresh insight and inspiration. To keep ourselves and our ideas fresh and vital, we must venture out from the confinement of our classrooms and sample what other people and places are up to.

Similarly, we have to be constantly on guard against narrowness. There is a natural tendency to stay with the familiar and comfortable, with ideas that we agree with, and with people who share our ideas and values. New ideas and people who are "different" may make us feel uncomfortable. However, this kind of narrowness only restricts our personal growth, which involves deciding what we believe—which brings us back to philosophy. If we know what we believe, if we have developed a sound philosophic base, we should not feel uncomfortable or threatened by ideas and people who are different from ourselves. Instead, we should embrace these opportunities for learning.

About Living With Ambiguity

A creating classroom holds many ambiguities and unanswered questions, and these will often challenge you. However, the experience will help you discover how independent and competent you are, and you will discover your best thinking patterns and problem-solving techniques.

Nevertheless, moving beyond the comfortable or secure can be frightening. Attempting new things introduces us to ourselves as learners—certainly an important task for teachers. We are not often encouraged to take such risks, but we should risk anyway. In so doing, we will force ourselves to think, to create, to learn, and thus to model for our students. Our own education should be as dynamic as that of our students.

About Valuing Beauty in the Classroom

Often our students are not exposed to much beauty in their lives. If awareness of beauty is not developed in children, how will they cope with the many unpleasant realities they will face as adults? What better time to craft that important facet into their lives? Although some teachers may get stalled on the philosophical questions of "what is beauty" and "who decides," the fact that "beauty is in the eye of the beholder" should not paralyze us into doing nothing. Most of us would agree on many things of beauty, such as fresh flowers for a bouquet, or music by Mozart or Beethoven. Let's expose our students to elements such as these!

On Tour Day, the students and I set up a table with a white table cloth, fresh flowers, cake, punch, and coffee. It was interesting to watch the students' response. For many it was a new experience, and they loved setting it up and looking at it. They put on their best behavior and enjoyed an air of civility.

We should seek other opportunities for students to create and observe beauty. Aren't there other occasions for a bouquet of flowers in the classroom, or a beautiful piece of artwork? We should also make time for field trips to the art gallery, the museum, the philharmonic, and the botanical gardens. Yes, there are many ways to polish these facets.

About Philosophy

Occasionally I hear people make a remark such as "What good is philosophy? I'm a practical person." This kind of statement reveals someone who doesn't understand what philosophy is all about—understanding what you believe. What could be more practical than knowing what you believe?

In the era in which we live, the era of "more and faster," it is well worth taking time out to examine and write down for ourselves what we believe. It will be both frustrating and enlightening, but very beneficial. It might even help us feel a new surge of renewal as we recapture some of our lost idealism.

This experience should help clarify why we do many of the things we do, but it can also reveal that some of those things are inconsistent with our beliefs. What a blow that is! However, it is important to bring into focus what we believe, and it is much easier to orchestrate the classroom when we are working from a well-thought-out philosophy. The students won't be getting mixed messages, and we won't feel so distracted. And best of all, we may find a well-thought-out reason for saying "no" to certain things.

Writing a personal life philosophy is a difficult task. It takes reflection, thinking, and erasing. However, once you've reflected and put onto paper what you truly believe about learning, children, curriculum, and society, life shouldn't seem so confusing or cluttered. It will take quite a while, but it probably will be one of the most worthwhile activities you'll ever do. Of course, a philosophy is not necessarily permanent. It can change with new ideas and new thoughts, or it may not.

The hardest part is practicing what you believe. If you follow through in this, you may eliminate many of the tasks you presently peform, and you may revolutionize the way you teach. Accept the challenge! You may discover that time is too valuable to spend on shuffling papers, sitting in boring committee meetings, or other busywork.

About Setting Expectations

I am old-fashioned when it comes to expecting students to get their work done. When an assignment is due, I expect it to be done—done well, and on schedule. I believe that if I help my students develop productive work habits, self-discipline, and pride in accomplishment, I have given them the best of all lessons and the most precious of all gifts. The ability to see any task to completion is indeed worthwhile. The nature of project activities requires a good measure of self-discipline on the part of students, since much of the work is long-term and is done independently. It would be ideal if students could acquire this habit before they begin the project, because things would certainly go much smoother. But the fact is that some students are dilatory and need a lot of encouragement, and sometimes outright prodding, to complete a task. On the other hand, the high level of excitement and motivation that a project can generate often provides a powerful impetus for students to develop productive work habits, self discipline, and pride in accomplishment.

Beware! There can also be a dark side to setting expectations in your classroom. This is the prejudging and labeling of students—expecting too much or too little of them, or expecting "Johnny" to misbehave because another teacher said that he was a trouble-maker. Prejudging doesn't benefit anyone, but it certainly can hurt. Would we like to be labeled for the rest of our lives because of the worst thing we did as children (or as adults)? Never having it forgotten? Never being able to change or be given a chance to make a new beginning? Of course, none of us would want to be trapped like that—and neither do children.

When we are open to messing around with ideas and materials, helping each other, learning together, and finding that there are many ways of solving problems, there is no place for labeling or prejudging, which only set up barriers to learning and creating. Not only must we avoid setting up such barriers for students, but we also must make sure that our students do not set up barriers for one another. No labeling by anyone! Just help, cooperation, and high expectations for everyone!

About Taking Care of Ourselves

There is a danger that by now the reader is convinced that I must have worked nonstop, like an efficient furnace generating twenty-four hours of heat each day. Be heartened, Reader; this was not the case. Instead, I had to pace myself and become selective in what I did, for it is too easy to dream more schemes and make more plans than you have the energy to accomplish.

We are an exhausted profession. There is too much stress, overwork, and bombardment. As teachers, we seldom have time to think something through, or collect our thoughts; we must react immediately, hundreds of times each day in the classroom. At the same time, we are expected to be lovable and perfect, all things to all people, and we are not supposed to make mistakes. Though we know this is an impossible, ludicrous expectation, we still may feel stress and self-doubt. It is possible to become bedazzled by the speedometer of the classroom at the expense of our physical and emotional endurance.

Project teaching can reduce stress by condensing the amount of work required during the school day. When working on a project, the students become responsible for much of their own learning. The teacher's responsibilities shift away from being the primary source of information to that of being a facilitator and co-learner. Under the demands of "normal" teaching, there is seldom time to reflect on what we are doing. Daily expectations can create a treadmill of overwhelming incidentals—of trying to be all things to all people. Furthermore, when we try to accomplish too many things, we are in danger of making much of what we do become superficial and meaningless to students. And it wears us out!

How can any of us accomplish anything important for ourselves, our students, or our world, when we become exhausted by incidentals? It is essential for us to slow down and focus on the things that seem most important. Focus on fewer things, but do them in depth. Depth is where real learning takes place, and it is less stressful on the teacher.

Burnout is a genuine and constant danger. Avoiding burnout requires daily renewal. It is important to recognize that there is life outside the classroom. Of course, it is necessary to take schoolwork home; that goes with the territory. However, we must keep it at a reasonable level and not let it dominate our private lives. It is essential to maintain other dimensions of living. Our home (and couch) should not be an annex to the classroom. Home should be primarily for family, relaxation, solitude, hobbies, friends, food, and conversation about something other than school. Come back to school each day refreshed, and you will feel better and get more accomplished in the classroom.

At the risk of sounding like a fussy mother, let me say a word about taking care of your physical self. We know that the body and mind function better when they get enough sleep, rest, exercise, and nutritious food. At the end of a hard day of teaching, it is easy to feel too tired to eat proper meals and to exercise. Believe me, you had best not fall into that trap. Lack of good food and exercise only assures that you will feel even more tired, your health will decline, your enthusiasm will wane, and your work will suffer. Teaching is too challenging to allow that to happen!

Closing Thoughts About Looking Back

Of course, we need to look back, in spite of what McLuhan and other futurists say, in order to reflect on our profession, our teaching, our successes and our failures. After all, reflection on experience is how we learn.

So, let's pause and take a good look. What have we done? What have we learned? Are we doing exactly the same things that we did five, ten, or twenty years ago? Have we changed? Has the change been growth? Let's hope so. The past is scattered with the mile posts that help us locate ourselves in the present, and by those same mile posts we set our sights to the future. So where do we go from here?

The past and the future are opposite directions on the same highway, and today we stand at the roadside looking both ways. While we set our sights for the future, we must also check the road behind us. We dare not move along that road too slowly, lest we be overtaken by another big and noisy road show. Another bandwagon? Another panacea? A genuine innovation? How will we know without reflecting on where we have been? After all, reflection on experience is how we learn.

Appendix A

Notes on the Washington, DC, Curriculum

*T*he Washington, DC, project was organized around the nation's capital and its symbols. This contrasts with the Latin America project, which was organized around the six strands of social studies: history, geography, government (political science), economics, sociology, and anthropology. The Washington, DC, project contained elements of the six strands of social studies, but these were not the organizing principle.

Because of the differences in organization and structure, the curriculum outline shown here in Appendix A necessarily differs from the outline found for the Latin America project in Appendix B. The learnings for the Washington, DC, project are listed under specific buildings and other features, whereas the learnings for the Latin America project are listed under the separate strands of social studies as generalizations and examples. These differences offer teachers two contrasting approaches for organizing a class project.

THE CAPITOL

Factual Learnings

1. Where the elected representatives of American people meet to write the national laws.
2. How the legislative branch of our government works.
3. About the story of Columbus on the bronze doors of the Capitol.
4. About different art forms and architecture.
5. Stories of some great Americans in Statuary Hall.
6. How history is interwoven through the art at the Capitol.
7. About the significance of the Statue of Freedom on the dome.

Integrated Learnings

1. *Social studies.* Students learned how our form of government works.
2. *Reading.* Students read textbooks, encyclopedias, library books, magazines, newspapers, and other printed materials.
3. *Writing/Language Arts.* Students wrote letters to the U.S. Senators and Representatives from Idaho. They learned to take notes.
4. *Art.* Students learned the different techniques of art used in the Capitol and about the many artists who made contributions.
5. *History.* Students learned history through the art and statuary of the Capitol.
6. *Math.* Students learned how high nineteen-and-one-half feet is (from the Statue of Freedom) and began to estimate feet.

Our U.S. Senators and Representatives work in this building, and as the students began learning how our form of government works, we wrote to our Congressmen for information and received excellent replies.

Larry Craig, one of Idaho's U.S. Representatives (later a Senator), once visited our class on Tour Day and presented the class with a flag that had flown over the United States Capitol.

On Tour Day, every student could explain how the legislative branch of the government works. This was tied into our study of the Constitution, which we had learned about in the "before 1800" section.

However, there was much more to learn from the Capitol. The figure on top of the Capitol dome is the Statue of Freedom. She is an important symbol of our nation. We learned several symbols and what they stand for.

Statuary Hall is a memorial to great Americans. Each state is invited to place statues of two of its most famous people in the hall. We learned who the two people from Idaho were, and their significance to Idaho and the nation. We also learned about some of the other famous people, such as Robert Fulton, Roger Williams, Robert E. Lee, and Jefferson Davis. We had encountered Williams before 1800, and it was interesting to see him again. We talked about the others and their places after 1800.

Students are interested to see someone they've studied earlier in history pop up in a later time. They discover that ideas live through time. Some students decided to find out who all of the statues were and why their states chose to put them there. This kind of project lends itself to many open-ended research possibilities.

The Capitol has many paintings rich in history, and we also studied these. They included the *Emancipation Proclamation, Washington, Jefferson,* and *Hamilton, Washington at Yorktown, the Landing of Columbus,* and the *Declaration of Independence.* We included the Bronze Doors on the Capitol, which tell the story of Christopher Columbus, which we already knew. I found that using the art to review all of these historical events, which we had learned about earlier, was an excellent teaching device.

Each year, the student who built the Capitol included many of these details in its construction and design, and the top of the Capitol lifted off to show the rooms and artwork inside. Much of the information and the interrelationships involved were researched by that student, and he or she shared that knowledge in cooperative learning groups using jigsaw and other techniques. I taught many of the details to the whole class through conversations and discussions. All students were responsible for knowing all the information on Tour Day—and they did!

THE WHITE HOUSE

Factual Learnings

1. Where the President of the United States lives and works.
2. How the executive branch of our government works.
3. About the history of the White House. (The White House is the nation's house and is filled with history.)
4. How the White House was burned during the War of 1812.
5. That the Oval Office is the President's office.
6. That the Green Room is used to entertain guests.
7. That the Lincoln Bedroom is where President Lincoln signed the Emancipation Proclamation.
8. Why there is a helicopter landing pad.
9. About the Easter egg roll.

Integrated Learnings

History, government, literature, reading, writing, citizenship, current events

The White House ties in the executive branch of our government. The students learned about this branch of government when studying the Constitution. The White House helped them to see the President and his powers and duties in a more familiar light. They learned about his house, where he lives, and what he does for them as citizens. He became much more human.

The student who builds and designs the White House furnishes and decorates many of the rooms. The many historical pieces in the rooms make more connections in history for the students. For example, the Lincoln Bedroom makes links to the Civil War and the Emancipation Proclamation. A plaque on the fireplace mantel tells of that event. This also connects to Ford's Theatre, the Petersen House, and the Lincoln Memorial.

Kids love to learn about the Green Room. I don't know whether it is an important learning, but I do know that kids love this kind of information. For example, the First Lady entertains people there, the white marble mantel was brought from Italy in 1819, and the golden clock and vases on the mantel were ordered from France when James Monroe was President. The class and I find Italy and France on the map, and 1819 on the time line, and see what else was happening in the world besides someone bringing white marble to the White House. The students seem to use this kind of information to help remember the bigger, more important pieces, such as what the President of the United States does.

The helicopter landing pad and the Easter egg roll fall into the same category. Students like to learn that the Presidential helicopter lands on the White House lawn right at his door, and that it is piloted by a special Air Force officer who is ready at all times to whisk the President any place he wants to go. They are intrigued with the fact that no airplane except this helicopter can fly over or near the White House.

This kind of information makes for interesting discussions. Students connect these details to more difficult concepts such as the executive branch of the government and the powers and duties of the President. They seem to be able to recall and process information much more readily.

When we study the War of 1812, the students are always shocked to learn that the British burned Washington, DC, and the White House. It is something they don't forget.

It is always interesting after Easter to hear the students discussing what they saw on the news. The Easter egg roll! In addition to the bonus of seeing the White House, the students have found the pleasure of knowing about something in the news. This is a beginning for building an interest in current events, which in time will become more sophisticated.

Materials   Pieces of wallpaper and fabric will be needed for furnishing the rooms.

THE SUPREME COURT BUILDING

Factual Learnings

1. Where the Constitution, the law of our land, is interpreted.
2. The Supreme Court is made up of nine justices, one of whom is the Chief Justice.

3. How the judicial branch of our government works.
4. What the justices do.
5. How important decisions are made in a Supreme Court case.
6. About the importance of Sandra Day O'Conner as the first woman justice.
7. About the names of the current justices and their biographies.
8. How the court system works.
9. About the style of a Greek temple.

Integrated Learnings

Government, citizenship, architecture, stories of people, analyzing a court case, higher-level thinking, a mock trial

The Capitol, the White House, and the Supreme Court Building are the buildings that house the executive, the legislative, and the judicial branches of our government. Through the project process—construction, discussions, collaboration, research, and note taking—students gain a conceptual framework for the government and how it works.

When people take off the lid of the Supreme Court Building, they see nine justices making important decisions. When students take people on the tour of Washington, DC, they explain the workings of the three branches of government and the duties and powers of each.

THE NATIONAL ARCHIVES BUILDING

Factual Learnings

1. Where the Declaration of Independence is housed.
2. Where the Constitution is housed.
3. Where the Bill of Rights is housed.
4. How these three documents are interrelated, what they stand for, and what they mean for all Americans.
5. How these three documents are guarded more closely than the President of the United States.
6. How these documents can be viewed by the public during the day.

Integrated Learnings

Government, history, citizenship, Thomas Jefferson and other Founding Fathers

The students have previously learned what the Declaration of Independence is, who wrote it, and why it is important—and they have learned to recite the first sentence. They also know the parts of the Constitution, particularly those referring to the executive, legislative, and judicial branches. They have studied the Bill of Rights, can name all ten amendments, and can discuss how each of these relates to their lives and those of their families. During the tour, they discuss all of these facets with their tour guests.

When people lift off the lid of the National Archives Building, they see tiny facsimiles of these documents. The students are fascinated to learn that we still have these documents from ages ago, that they are preserved in a metal and glass case, and that during the day the case is always protected by a special guard. And they love to discover that at night this case is lowered through the floor into a fireproof, bomb-proof vault beneath the building. There is always a lot of speculation about how this could be simulated for the tour. I like this kind of discussion among students.

Thomas Jefferson enters the conversation about the National Archives when the Declaration of Independence and the Bill of Rights are discussed.

THE JEFFERSON MEMORIAL

Factual Learnings

1. About Thomas Jefferson as a man of many talents.
2. How Thomas Jefferson has influenced all of our lives.
3. How the memorial is magnificent because of its beautiful architecture.
4. About some of Jefferson's words and thoughts that are carved around the walls of the memorial.

Integrated Learnings

History, science, architecture, art, aesthetics, Thomas Jefferson

Most textbooks today neglect the human side of our historic figures. This is truly a great loss for our children, because only if we can bond students to the humanity of our forefathers will our history, government, cultural values, and civic responsibility come alive.

Thomas Jefferson is almost an entire curriculum all by himself. Not only was he a great statesman and one of our key Founding Fathers, he was a person of many talents. When the students "meet" Thomas Jefferson, they get acquainted with our second Vice-President, our third President, the writer of the Declaration of Independence, and the founder of the University of Virginia—all in one person. Since they live in Idaho, my students, are fascinated that it was Jefferson who sent the explorers Lewis and Clark west, through Idaho, to the Pacific Ocean.

The students also learn that Jefferson was a writer, a scientist, an inventor, and an architect. We study some of his writings and talk about the attributes of a good writer.

Jefferson provides a natural means to introduce science into the project. As a student, Jefferson studied mathematics and science, and became interested in nature and how things work. What is more, Jefferson used his mathematical and scientific knowledge to build his home, Monticello. In later life, he invented the steel plow, which made farming easier, and he invented many devices in Monticello that made life easier and more pleasant. He also collected fossils and animal specimens that were of scientific interest to him.

By hearing about Monticello, students learn what being an architect means, and how Jefferson used this skill to design his famous home. This naturally leads to talking about design and learning about sketching our buildings. Scale and perspective become topics of conversation, and we use this new knowledge when we begin our project.

Though presented here in limited detail, each of the following buildings and structures carries its own factual and integrated learnings. The teacher can develop these using the examples given earlier.

MONTICELLO

Thomas Jefferson's house is a wonderful part of the project even though it is located near Charlottesville, Virginia, not in Washington, DC. The house personifies Jefferson; throughout are reminders of his intellect and interests. Today, the entrance hall is a museum containing fossil bones, a buffalo head, elk antlers, and a seven-day clock. The house shows Jefferson's love of architecture, and the grounds portray his love of horticulture.

Monticello provided a wonderful opportunity for students to begin the study of plants. Jefferson tested over 250 varieties of vegetables and herbs, and many of these varieties are grown today in his one-thousand-foot vegetable garden. Monticello brought us closer to knowing Thomas Jefferson and his contributions to mankind.

MOUNT VERNON

Mount Vernon, the home of George Washington, is on the outskirts of Washington, DC. This gave us another opportunity to study a great American and how he lived.

Both Monticello and Mount Vernon were impressive buildings for our project. Both models were built with roofs that came off to show the rich detail of the homes. These two homes seemed to be unifying points for much of the history of the period.

THE SMITHSONIAN INSTITUTION

Smithsonian Buildings and Exhibits Used in the Project

National Museum of Natural History
National Gallery of Art—East Building
National Gallery of Art—West Building
Hirshhorn Museum and Sculpture Garden
Kennedy Center for the Performing Arts

National Museum of American History
Arts and Industries Building
National Air and Space Museum
The Castle
National Zoological Park (National Zoo)

The buildings and exhibits of the Smithsonian Institution provide wonderful material for integration of all areas you could hope to teach. The Smithsonian operates the most fascinating collection of museums in the world, which are sometimes dubbed "the attic of our nation." They are certainly an excellent source for teaching science, geography, multiculturalism, anthropology, math, art, and probably anything else.

The main group of Smithsonian buildings is located between the Capitol and the Washington Monument. The Kennedy Center and the National Zoo are located in other parts of the city.

The National Museum of Natural History

The National Museum of Natural History has fossil displays and exhibits of African, Asian, Pacific, and Native American cultures. It also has earth, moon, and meteorite displays; exhibits on the people of North and South America; and an insect zoo. There are mineral exhibits, and the blue Hope Diamond is on display. Students love the story of the Hope diamond and all the tragedies that occurred to its many owners. In addition, there are exhibits relating to human cultures, mammals, birds, amphibians, reptiles, sea life, insects, plants, rocks, and gems.

As we work on the project, I teach specific science lessons from the topics related to the Smithsonian. The student who designs and builds the National Museum of Natural History includes all of the displays that we study, so when students lift off the roof, all of this information is included for tour guests.

Often the student who builds this building will study and include science topics other than the ones I have taught. This is a real advantage to project teaching—students often become intrigued by something new to them, and they discover the pleasure of pursuing a topic just because it interests them. I always hope that this experience will inspire yet another generation of lifetime learners.

The National Gallery of Art— East Building

Too often, art in school merely has meant students coloring something chosen by the teacher, or at best, students being told to make a picture. Art is much more than this, and even a teacher with no special art training can develop excellent lessons in art by using carefully chosen topics.

The art galleries of the Smithsonian can provide a new focus for the students' and the teacher's thinking. The Smithsonian can provide two different kinds of art to study in school: the study of architectural design and of the national art treasures themselves.

Architectural Design   The East Building is interesting because of its design. It consists of two triangular sections built to fit on the trapezoidal shape of the property. This is wonderful material for math discussions about such ideas as "If property is this shape, what kind of building would you design?" I usually taught my geometry unit, incorporating the idea of art and architectural design, while building Washington, DC.

National Art Treasures   Why shouldn't students become acquainted with Henri Matisse and his paper cut-outs exhibited in the East Building, or the several pieces of large sculpture? Some students have been interested in trying these techniques. Sometimes the student designing the East Building has written to the Smithsonian to find out what special exhibits would be shown during the time of the project. Then the student could research those artists so that some of their works could be displayed with the project. Small versions of the artwork would be placed inside the model of East Building.

The National Gallery of Art— West Building

The National Gallery of Art consists of two buildings: the newer East Building and the older West Building. The West Building houses an excellent collection of European and American painting and sculpture from the thirteenth century to the present. The students can become acquainted with famous artists such as Raphael, Van Eyck, Rembrandt, and Vermeer. The architecture of this building is an interesting contrast to the newer East Building, and this makes a good discussion topic. Students explore why building styles change, their own reasons for preferring one over another, what would influence such different styles, and whether the two different styles are compatible with one another.

The Hirshhorn Museum This is rather an interesting museum from my view point; it seems no one is sure how to spell it. Some books spell it with a *c* and others don't. Students who have never looked for information are suddenly riffling through all the material to see how it is spelled. Also, the shape of the building is round and looks ready for take-off—which intrigues students. The round shape provides a nice reason to work on circumference in math. It also contains interesting nineteenth- and twentieth- century American art, which I like to introduce to students.

The Kennedy Center for the Performing Arts The Kennedy Center provides wonderful entertainment, drawing talent from all around the country and the world. There are two great hallways that lead from the Entrance Plaza to the Grand Foyer. The Hall of States flies the flags of all the states and territories. The Hall of Nations flies the flags of more than one hundred countries recognized by the United States.

Students are fascinated with flags, so here is a fine opportunity to capitalize on their interests. Students research the flags of the states, territories, and countries represented at the Kennedy Center and make small replicas for this building. In the process, their geographical skills are enhanced. Often the student designing the Kennedy Center enlists help from the class for the flags.

The students are also interested in John F. Kennedy because he is much closer in time to them. It is important to include significant people all along the timeline of our history.

The National Museum of American History Here is another treasure trove for learning. Look at the things you can introduce and teach to students! The Foucault Pendulum at the center of the lobby demonstrates the movement of the earth—a wonderful science discussion. Many other exhibits relate to the history of science and technology. On display are farm machinery and railroad vehicles from the late 1800s, as well as horse-drawn wagons from the 1700s.

There are exhibits of ship models, steam engines, and bridge and tunnel construction. The Hall of Electricity displays the inventions of Benjamin Franklin, Samuel Morse, Alexander Bell, and Thomas Edison. Other exhibits include the equipment used in the study of geology, oceanography, and meteorology.

The second floor has wonderful displays of social and political history. For example, exhibits include the First Ladies' Gowns, a collection of White House china, and displays of American Life in the past. There are exhibits that explore politics and government and the convergence of diverse cultures.

The third floor has collections of rare stamps, antique ceramics, glass, money, medals, and musical instruments.

The original Star Spangled Banner proudly hails in this building. One of our most interesting national symbols, this flag flew over Ft. McHenry during its famous bombardment by the British in 1814. The student who designs this building has a miniature replica of the tattered flag hanging on display for those who remove the roof. This relic is connected to the topic of the War of 1812 and the writing of a poem by Francis Scott Key that eventually became our national anthem, "The Star Spangled Banner," which we learn to sing. The mind boggles at such a wealth of interesting information to study. This is where you must truly be a decision maker.

The National Air and Space Museum

This has become the most popular museum at the Smithsonian since its opening in 1976 and is just as intriguing for fifth graders to design and to study. One exhibit focuses on astronomy, which provides another excellent tie-in for science.

Highlights for tourists and students include Lindbergh's Spirit of St. Louis, the Wright Brothers' Kitty Hawk, John Glenn's Friendship 7, the Apollo 11 Command Module, and the Viking Lander. We also learn about the people involved and their accomplishments. The student who builds the National Air and Space Museum includes replicas of these exhibits inside the building.

This building contains a variety of aircraft, spacecraft, missiles, rockets, balloons, military aviation, and flight equipment. The exhibits are of great interest to many of the students, and I found that they pursued much of this information on their own after I introduced the possibilities.

The history of flight is an approach to history that often appeals to otherwise history-shy students. Beryl Markham's flight is an interesting event to connect with Lindberg's flight. In 1936, Beryl Markham became the first person to fly solo across the Atlantic from east to west, taking off in England and crash-landing in Nova Scotia. Students like to contrast this with Lindberg's solo flight from west to east, and they trace both routes on the world map.

Whenever you can add human interest stories for discussion, be sure to do it. Students like stories about real people and their adventures, and I found that the more stories that were woven into the project, the easier it was for students to remember important information.

The Castle The Castle is the oldest Smithsonian building. The story of James Smithson, an English scientist who donated over a half million dollars to the United States for building the Smithsonian, is fascinating. I read this story to the students during the project. Also, the Castle architecture is interesting and adds variety to the other buildings of the Smithsonian. Since so much of Washington, DC, is white, it is a relief to have something with color on the floor.

The National Zoological Park We also included the National Zoological Park, commonly called the National Zoo. It is an excellent vehicle for the study of science and geography. And what an interesting place for students to study! The zoo publishes a map that we used for mapping skills. The student who designed the zoo had to figure out from the map where all the animals belong, and then put them in the right spots. Most of the class got involved in this activity. They studied the map and the directions and tried to find the exact spot for the reptiles or pandas or whatever.

The zoo provides a wonderful connection for the study of animals and the places in the world that they come from. We did a lot of research on the Giant Pandas given to President Nixon—where the pandas came from, and what China, their part of the world, was like. Environmental concerns entered the conversations as we discovered that the Giant Pandas' natural environment is disappearing, and that there are fewer than one thousand pandas left in existence.

OTHER BUILDINGS, EXHIBITS AND FEATURES

Now that you have an idea of the way I organized the important learnings and integration for each building and exhibit we used, I will give a shorter review of other buildings, exhibits, and features. I have omitted a number of interesting possibilities, but surely your interest would wane after reading the seventy-seventh item on the list.

The actual number of buildings and exhibits used varied with the number of students in the class, and with specific interests that students had. You may well find others that you wish to use.

The National Geographic Society Building

Students love this building when they are introduced to it. This is the headquarters of the world's largest scientific organization. The Society has several million members who receive the *National Geographic* magazine each month. By now, the students are very aware of the *National Geographic* magazine and have used it daily for our project. This is a wonderful building to emphasize geography, science, and the habit of reading the *National Geographic*.

The student who designs this building learns that the world's largest unmounted globe of the earth is displayed here. A replica of the giant globe goes into the model of the building. Explorer's Hall in the National Geographic Building displays a huge map of the world as explorers first saw it in 1651, during the Age of Discovery. This is also sketched into the model.

The Library of Congress

The Library of Congress is the largest and most complete library in the world. The first Library of Congress was located in the Capitol, but it was destroyed when the British burned the Capitol in 1814. The government then bought Thomas Jefferson's personal library of six thousand books, which was the beginning of the present library.

One student, who was designing the Library of Congress, made a long-distance call to the Library to find out the color of the dome and the texture of the building. What a wonderful learning experience! Another student did a survey of the students in the class to find out their favorite books. He then made a shelf that included the names of these books and placed it inside the Library. Then he included all of his own favorites on another shelf.

Building the Library of Congress seemed to inspire students to do research. Another student set out to find the titles of the six thousand books that Jefferson sold to the library. I don't know if her search is over, but I'm hoping to hear from her.

Last but not least, this building is another wonderful tie-in to Thomas Jefferson, as well as the War of 1812.

The Washington Monument

This giant obelisk stands at the end of the Mall opposite from the Capitol, and it can provide several good lessons in math, geometry, history, and geography. It is shaped like the obelisks of ancient Egypt, but several times larger. It's height is 555 feet, 5-1/8 inches, and each side is 55 feet, 1-1/8 inches at the base. It is hollow, with 898 steps leading to the top. Students are very interested in the Washington Monument, for it provides many interesting facts and connections.

The Lincoln Memorial

This impressive memorial is visited by more people than any other in the world. It is designed much like a Greek Temple. The thirty-six great columns represent the thirty-six states that were in the Union when Lincoln died. When we study this memorial, we study about Abraham Lincoln and the Civil War.

Connections include the Lincoln Bedroom at the White House, Ford's Theatre, and the Petersen House where Lincoln died. The students also read and discuss the Gettysburg Address and his Second Inaugural Address. When students stop at this memorial on the tour, they describe the life of Lincoln and his influence in government, and discuss the two speeches. They also talk about the Civil War and Lincoln's role in it.

Ford's Theatre

Ford's Theatre is the site where John Wilkes Booth assassinated President Lincoln while the President was watching "Our American Cousin" on April 14, 1865. It has since been restored and is now an operating theatre. The model of the theatre is designed to show the President's Box and the flags inside the building.

The Petersen House

President Lincoln was carried to this house after being shot at the Ford's Theatre. Mrs. Lincoln waited the night in the front parlor. Lincoln died the following morning at 7:22. This building has a much different design than many of the official buildings, and adds a counterpoint. Students who design this building and Ford's Theatre become experts on the life of Lincoln.

Arlington House—the Custis-Lee Mansion

Arlington House is the Robert E. Lee National Memorial. This mansion seems to bring together the drama and tragedy of the Civil War. It was once the home of General Robert E. Lee, who became commanding general of all the Confederate armies after he turned down President Lincoln's offer to appoint him field commander of the Union Army. Mrs. Lee and her family had to abandon the mansion during the Civil War. Following the surrender of the Confederate forces at Appomattox Courthouse, Lee and his family never returned to his home, which he had called Arlington. Later, he became President of the college that is now known as Washington and Lee University.

The land surrounding Arlington House was first used for army camp sites, and later was set aside for the burial of soldiers. The land was designated Arlington National Cemetery in 1864. The story of Arlington House provides material for a study of the Civil War and the many ramifications. Arlington National Cemetery is included in the project, together with the Tomb of the Unknowns, and the grave site of John F. Kennedy. I discuss and teach the meaning of all of these memorials.

The Tomb of the Unknowns

In Arlington National Cemetery lie three American heroes, one from each of three wars—World War I, World War II, and the Korean War. The inscription reads, "Here rests in honored glory an American soldier known but to God." I don't go into much depth about these wars, but we do mark them on the time line in order to put them into perspective chronologically.

The Pentagon

The Pentagon is the headquarters of the United States Department of Defense, and is one of the largest office buildings in the world. It is almost a city in itself; the Capitol Building could fit into any one of its five wedge-shaped sections. Such comparisons interest students. The Pentagon is tied to the duties of the President, who is Commander-in-Chief of the Armed Services. In turn, this provides an opportunity for the students to learn about our nation's defense system.

Last but not least, the geometric shape of the Pentagon lends itself to another geometry lesson.

The Bureau of Printing and Engraving

This is where money is printed, as well as all other items of financial character issued by the United States government. This building is the tie-in for the teaching of economics and why we print money. Most students are interested in money!

The Washington Cathedral

Washington Cathedral serves as an opportunity to teach about the separation of state and religion in our country. The students have already learned that part of our country was settled by colonists looking for religious freedom. We don't study religion as a subject; instead, we study about the importance of religion to people, and the influences it has had on our country. Martin Luther King and other religious/political activists enter into these discussions.

The Washington Cathedral is based on fourteenth-century French and English Gothic style. We study what a cathedral is, when and why they originated, the architecture, and who it serves. The student designing this building (which certainly is not an easy task) includes the Rose Window and the gargoyles and grotesques.

The Rose Window is an excellent example of stained glass. There are more than nine thousand pieces of stained glass in the window, and to everyone's surprise, there is embedded in it a piece of moon rock brought back to earth by the astronauts of Apollo 11. There are many interesting interrelationships in this window, as with the entire cathedral, and many connections with previous knowledge.

Gargoyles and grotesques are perched on the outside of the Cathedral. The students are intrigued to learn that these monsters were put up by the builders to keep rain water from flowing down the limestone walls and staining them.

One year, for an art project, each student pretended to be a stone carver and designed a creature for the Cathedral. We also did research to see why stone creatures first appeared on European cathedrals about eight hundred years ago.

The Potomac River and the Tidal Basin

We couldn't have Washington, DC, without the Potomac River and the Tidal Basin. The Potomac and the Tidal Basin always included many trees with pink blossoms, and the students learned the story of the cherry trees. Students made their own cherry tree designs, and I often marveled at how many different ways one could make a cherry tree.

Dulles International Airport

Dulles International Airport is located twenty-seven miles from Washington. This airport has an unusual design, so we discussed the architecture of the building. We also discussed why people from all over the world fly in and out of Dulles. This is a good incentive to teach about why there are different time zones and how to calculate them.

Theodore Roosevelt Island

This island in the Potomac River contains a modest memorial to President Theodore Roosevelt. The entire island is dedicated to him and his love of the wilderness.

The Vietnam Veterans Memorial

For a number of years, many students had heard of the Vietnam Veterans Memorial because it was shown a great deal on TV. The story of Maya Lin, the young woman who designed the memorial, always interested the students.

Blair House

This is the Vice-President's house. We included it whenever more buildings were needed.

The FBI Building

This building contains some interesting crime detection technology. Several students have been fascinated by it.

The Watergate Building

This large building complex was of considerable interest during the 1970s, following the resignation of President Nixon.

Washington National Airport

This busy airport is located along the Potomac River in Virginia, just across the river from Washington, DC.

Appendix B

Notes on the Latin America Curriculum

Whereas the Washington, DC, project was organized around the nation's capital and its symbols, the Latin America project was built upon the six strands of social studies: history, geography, government (political science), economics, sociology, and anthropology. The Washington, DC, project contained elements of the six strands of social studies, but they were not the organizing principle.

Because of the differences in organization and structure, the curriculum outline shown here in Appendix B necessarily differs from the outline found in Appendix A. Rather than being listed under specific buildings and other features, the learnings for the Latin America project are listed under the separate strands as generalizations and examples. These differences offer two contrasting approaches for organizing a class project. The generalizations listed here are examples of learnings that students should gain from the project.

SAMPLE GENERALIZATIONS ABOUT LATIN AMERICA

History

1. Great and ancient Indian civilizations of Mayans, Incas, and Aztecs had developed before the arrival of the Europeans.

2. Soon after the arrival of Columbus, Europeans began exploring and settling in Latin America.
3. Great numbers of Indians died during their early encounters with Europeans, both through warfare and from diseases brought by Europeans.
4. Because of the depopulation of Indian people due to warfare and disease, African slaves were brought to Latin America to provide labor for plantations and ranches.
5. Many wars were fought by the people of Latin America to gain their independence from the European nations.
6. Today's Latin American countries are independent and are peopled by the descendants of those earlier Indians, Europeans, and Africans, plus other groups who came later.

Geography

1. Latin America is a huge land area that includes South America, Central America, the Caribbean Islands, and part of North America.
2. Latin America contains land features that are among the most varied in the world—immense mountain ranges, huge rain forests, great deserts, vast prairies, great rivers, seemingly endless coastlines, and many islands.
3. Latin America is organized into many countries, which contain millions of people and many large cities.
4. The nature of the landscape influences the way people live.
5. The human activities involved in building a civilization—building cities, mining, manufacturing, farming—produce important changes in the natural environment.
6. The immense diversity of Latin America has created many kinds of regions.
7. Present-day Latin America is the result of a long history of movement of people and ideas.

Government

1. The Mayans, Incas, and Aztecs each had their own kind of efficient and effective government.

2. Europeans brought their own governmental systems and imposed them as they explored and settled in Latin America.
3. Several forms of government are represented in present-day Latin America.

Economics

1. The Indian peoples of Latin America had elaborate and successful trading systems prior to the coming of the Europeans. Their monetary systems differed from those in Europe.
2. The European pursuit of wealth and trade resulted in the voyage on which Columbus accidentally encountered the islands of the Caribbean while seeking a route to Asia.
3. Slaves were brought to Latin America to work on plantations that produced wealth for Europeans. Without slaves, early plantations would not have been profitable.
4. Today many of the foods and other products we use come from Latin America.

Sociology

1. The Indian civilizations of Latin America were well organized and highly developed.
2. The social systems of the Latin American Indians differed from one another, from those of the Europeans, and from those of Indian groups in the United States and Canada.
3. Group membership is important to the people of Latin America, including family, community, church, and political groups.

Anthropology

1. Each group—Indian, European, and African—represented a number of different languages, making communication difficult.
2. Each of these groups had different customs and beliefs.
3. Many early Indian traditions and customs continue to be practiced today.
4. Modern Latin America has a number of different cultures.

5. The cultures of Latin America have made many contributions to the United States and to the rest of the world.
6. The languages of Europe were adopted in Latin America. Most Latin American people today speak Spanish, but many speak Portuguese, and others speak French, Dutch, or English. Many Indians still speak their own native languages.

SAMPLE TOPICS AND LEARNINGS FOR THE SIX STRANDS OF SOCIAL STUDIES

History

Sample topics   The people and places listed below each possess a strong historical focus, though they are also connected to other strands. Individual student projects included one or more people or places. Some topics are connected (such as Aedes aegypti, Carlos Finley, and the Panama Canal), and would be part of a single project. Many students had more than one individual project, the actual number depending on the depth and complexity of the information available. The following can be identified as history topics, though many are also listed under other strands:

Aedes aegypti (mosquito)	Carlos Finley (Dr.)
Andrew Selkirk	Daniel Defoe's Imaginary Island
Atahualpa	Devil's Island
Aztec	Diego Rivera
Bernardo O'Higgins	Easter Island (related to research of Thor Heyerdahl)
Blackbeard	
Brasília	El Dorado
Cacao	Falkland Islands
Cape Horn	Galapagos Islands
Captain Dreyfus	Hispaniola
Captain Kidd	Inca
Columbus	Isthmus of Panama
Conquistadors	Iturbide
Cortés	Machu Picchu
Cusco	Magellan

Maya

Mexico City

Monroe Doctrine

Montezuma

Pampa

Panama Canal and Locks

Patagonian Express

Pizarro

Polynesia (related to research of
   Thor Heyerdahl)

San Martin

Símon Bolívar

Tenochtitlán

Thor Heyerdahl

Toussaint L'Ouverture

Sample of integrating history learnings: The Aedes aegypti mosquito

The Aedes aegypti mosquito is used here to illustrate how the history topics were used to integrate related learnings. After the student did research, messed around with ideas, built, talked, interviewed, and prepared for Tour Day, he or she could typically discuss many of the following topics, ranging from simple facts to complex issues:

How the Aedes aegypti affected the history of Latin America.

Why it was important to control malaria and yellow fever on the Isthmus of Panama.

What scientific and medical knowledge assisted in controlling these diseases.

Who was mainly responsible for overcoming the diseases.

Which countries were interested in building the Panama Canal and why.

The story of building the Panama Canal—the players and the drama.

What the Panama Canal does and how its locks work.

Why the Panama Canal was important to the rest of the world.

How important the Panama Canal is today.

Problems of big ships and the present canal.

Treaties that control the Panama Canal.

Geography

The five themes of geography

The study of geography has been organized into five themes by the Association of American Geographers and the National Council for Geographic Education. The geography studied during the Latin America project encompassed all five themes, developing each one when appropriate. The Five Themes of Geography are as follows:

Location (Absolute and Relative)   *Location* is the answer to the question, "Where?" *Absolute location* refers to the exact location on the earth's surface. Latitude and longitude are often used to express absolute location. *Relative location* is defined as location as related to some other feature or location. A description of the Amazon River as flowing east across northern Brazil is an example of relative location, whereas locating the mouth of the Amazon as 0° latitude and 50° west longitude is an example of absolute location.

Place (Physical and Human Characteristics)   *Place* is identified by special features that distinguish one location from another. For example, the Atacama Desert in Chile is distinguished physically as being arid with a warm climate (not hot) and rich in minerals. Its human characteristics include a sparse population.

Human-Environment Interactions (Relationships Within Places) There is constant interaction between people and their environment, and this makes changes both in the environment and in people's lives. For example, the Aztecs dug up soil from shallow lakes and used it to build small islands that were used for growing crops. This changed the nature of the lakes, but it also produced enough food to permit people to live in towns and cities instead of small villages where nearly everyone grew their own food. Today the efficient production of food permits people to live in towns and cities, but it changes the environment wherever that food is grown.

Movement (Mobility of People, Goods, and Ideas)   It's now a cliche that the globe has become smaller because of rapid and mass communication and travel. People have always traveled, communicated, and traded goods. As they travel and communicate, they exchange information and ideas. Thus goods and ideas spread throughout the world.

Chile is an excellent example of a country that could not exist without travel and communication. It stretches 2,650 miles north and south, and only 225 miles east and west. Good communication and transportation are essential to carry out the functions of government and the distribution of food and other goods and services.

Regions (Physical and Human)   A region is an area of land that can be identified by certain characteristics. A region may be defined by the physical characteristics of the land, or by the human activities that dominate the area. The Pampa of Argentina is a good example of a physical region. This is a large, grassy, fertile plain that covers about one-fifth of Argentina. On the other hand, the sugar cane fields around Salta and Tucuman form a human region—an area unified by the production of sugar.

Sample geography topics   The following geography features were used to identify location and place, which were physical and visible pieces of the project. However, this does not mean that geography stops there. The students should be encouraged to think like geographers, utilizing all five themes. While a student might typically think of his or her project as "the Panama Canal," in fact this is merely the focus for a much broader study, which includes all five themes of geography and all six strands of social studies.

The individual project became a focus for motivation, research, critical thinking, and problem solving. Though the items are geography topics, most have strong connections to history, government, economics, sociology, and anthropology—and thus are natural items for integration. As the students carried out research and constructed individual projects, their learnings flowed together and integrated with other areas of geography and social studies.

Although the following topics are identified here with geography, a number are also listed under other strands:

Amazon Rain Forest	Daniel Defoe's Imaginary Island
Andes Mountains	Devil's Island
Angel Falls	Easter Island (related to
Antilles, Lesser and Greater	research of Thor Heyerdahl)
Atacama Desert	El Dorado
Bahamas	Falkland Islands
Bermuda Triangle	Galapagos Islands
Brasília	Grenada
Buenos Aires	Lake Maracaibo
Cape Horn	Lake Titicaca
Christ of the Andes	Machu Picchu
Cusco	Mexico City

Orinoco River	Rio de Janeiro
Pampa	Santiago
Panama Canal	São Paulo
Peru/Humboldt Current	Strait of Magellan
Polynesia (related to research of	Sugar Loaf Mountain
Thor Heyerdahl)	Tenochtitlán
Popocatepetl	Trinidad
Quito	Veracruz

Sample of integrating geography learnings: The Amazon rain forest

The Amazon rain forest is used here to illustrate how the geography topics were used to integrate related learnings. After the student did research, messed around with ideas, built, talked, interviewed, and prepared for Tour Day, he or she could typically discuss many of the following topics, ranging from simple facts to complex issues.

Where the Amazon rain forest is located.

What identifies a forest as being a rain forest.

What all tropical rain forests have in common.

What the climate and weather are like.

What animals and plants are found there.

Why the Amazon River is important to the rain forest.

Why the Amazon River is important to the people who live there.

Who lives in the Amazon rain forest.

How the tropical rain forest affects the way these people live.

What effect these people have on the rain forest.

How and why the Amazon rain forest is changing.

How the culture and beliefs of the people of the rain forest differ
    from those of other people of Latin America.

How the lives of these people differ from the way people live in
    other regions, such as the Pampa or the Atacama Desert.

How the people of the Amazon rain forest interact with other peo-
    ple and other cultures.

Why the Amazon rain forest is important to the other people of Brazil.

Why the Amazon rain forest is important to people in other parts
    of the world.

Why scientists are interested in the Amazon rain forest.

The problems caused by cutting down the Amazon rain forest.

The problems caused if people stopped cutting down the Amazon
    rain forest.

Government

Sample topics   The study of government is inescapably interwoven with all of the other strands of social studies but is often ignored in the social studies curriculum. For example, the history and movement of people is related to specific governmental activities. Government controls economic activity, and economic activity controls government. Government is intrinsically bound to the culture and social structures of the people. Teachers need to become more aware of the connections of government to the various topics being studied. Students need opportunities to compare and contrast many forms of government.

Each of the following items has a relationship to the study of government, as well as ties to history, geography, and the other strands of social studies. A number of the items are also listed under other strands:

Atahualpa	Maya
Aztec	Mexico City
Brasília	Monroe Doctrine
Captain Dreyfus	Montezuma
Cusco	Panama Canal
Devil's Island	Símon Bolívar
Falkland Islands	Tenochtitlán
Hispaniola	Toussaint L'Ouverture
Inca	

Sample of integrating government learnings: The Inca   The Inca Indians are used here to illustrate how government topics were used to integrate related learnings. After the student did research, messed around with ideas, built, talked, interviewed, and prepared for Tour Day, he or she could typically discuss many of the following topics, ranging from simple facts to complex issues:

Who the Inca were and where they lived.

What Inca cities were like.

The size of the Inca empire.

How the Inca government was organized and how it worked.

How the Inca governed such a large empire.

How the Inca government differed from those of the Aztec and the Maya.

How the Inca traveled and communicated throughout their
    empire.
How the Inca kept records.
How and what the Inca traded.
What happened to the Inca government.

Economics

Sample topics   Throughout their history, the people of Latin America have engaged in
various kinds of economic activity. The Aztec, Inca, and Maya Indians
each had their own system of trade and barter, and they traded for
goods produced by Indian groups who lived in distant places. Trade
was (and is) influenced by available natural resources, the need for
goods and services, encounters with other people, and the ease or difficulty of travel.

When Europeans arrived, they brought their own ideas of trade,
including the use of money and a powerful desire to accumulate gold
and silver. Latin America provides an opportunity to study the development of economic systems and their evolution into modern systems
of exchange.

Each of the following items has a strong connection to the study of
economics, as well as ties to the other strands of social studies. A number of the items are also listed under other strands:

Argentine beef	Cortés
Amazon Rain Forest	Cusco
Bahamas	El Dorado
Balsam of Peru	Gaucho
Bananas	Grenada
Blackbeard	Guano
Buenos Aires	Henequen
Cacao	Hispaniola
Captain Kidd	Inca
Chicle	Kapok
Coffee Plantation	Llamas
Columbus	Machete
Conquistadors	Magellan
Copper Mines	Mahogany

Mexico City
Pampa
Pan American Highway
Panama Canal
Panama Hats
Patagonian Express
Pizarro
Plantations
Quipu
Quito
Rio de Janeiro

Santiago
São Paulo
Sisal
Sugar Cane
Tin Mines
Tobago
Toussaint L'Ouverture
Trinidad
Venezuelan Oil
Yerba Maté

Sample of integrating economics learnings: Argentine beef   Argentine beef is used here to illustrate how economic topics were used to integrate related learnings. After the student did research, messed around with ideas, built, talked, interviewed, and prepared for Tour Day, he or she could typically discuss many of the following topics, ranging from simple facts to complex issues:

Where Argentina is located and its important resources.
Why Argentina is well suited to raising beef cattle.
What kinds of jobs beef production creates.
How beef production benefits all of Argentina.
How Argentine beef affects world trade.
Why food trends affect beef production.
What factors outside of Argentina affect the production of beef in Argentina.
How changing world markets affect Argentina.
The advantages and disadvantages of beef production over mining in Argentina.

Sociology

Sample topics   Sociology is the study of groups of people and the interactions of these groups. Latin America is the home of many separate groups of people, representing a variety of patterns of group membership. The social systems of the earlier Indian groups differed from one another, and differed from those of the Europeans. Patterns today differ from earlier patterns.

Because of the close relationship of sociology to anthropology, during the project these two strands were studied and taught in an integrated fashion through case studies. The students used the case studies to analyze and compare both cultural patterns and sociological patterns.

Each of the groups below has a strong element of sociology in addition to anthropology and the other strands of social studies. These are also listed under anthropology:

Aztec   Spaniards
Inca   People of the Amazon rain
Maya   forest
Mexican family (contemporary)

Sample of integrating sociology learnings: The Maya

The Maya Indians are used here to illustrate how sociology topics were used to integrate related learnings. After the student did research, messed around with ideas, built, talked, interviewed, and prepared for Tour Day, he or she could typically discuss many of the following sociological topics, ranging from simple facts to complex issues. Though integrated with anthropology, the examples below are presented to illustrate some of the sociological content:

Where the Maya lived and how they were organized into
    groups.
How family groups were organized.
How cities and villages were organized.
How city life differed from village life.
How the Maya were governed.
The relationship between government and religious authority.
The influence of religion on Maya life.

Anthropology

Sample topics

Anthropology is the study of culture and institutions. Latin America is the home of many cultures, some radically different from others. The earlier cultures of the Indians differed from one another, and differed from those of the Europeans. Elements of those earlier cultures exist today. As noted above, anthropology and sociology were taught in an integrated fashion through case studies.

The groups listed below are the same groups listed under sociology. Each has a strong element of anthropology in addition to sociology and the other strands of social studies:

Aztec

Inca

Maya

Mexican family (contemporary)

Spaniards

People of the Amazon rain forest

Sample of integrating anthropology learnings: The Maya

The Maya Indians are used here to illustrate how anthropology topics were used to integrate related learnings. After the student did research, messed around with ideas, built, talked, interviewed, and prepared for Tour Day, he or she could typically discuss many of the following cultural topics, ranging from simple facts to complex issues. Though integrated with sociology, the examples below are presented to illustrate some of the anthropological content.

What a Maya home was like.

How Maya people made a living.

What Maya people ate and wore.

How Maya people adorned themselves.

The nature of Mayan language.

Mayan mathematics and science.

The nature of Mayan art.

The nature of Mayan religious rituals and ceremonies.

Games the Maya people played.

Mysteries of the Mayan civilization.

Appendix C

Things to Do—A Project Guide

*T*he following tasks are reminders of things that need to be done. They are listed in phases, not step-by-step, because the process is flexible and certain items may be optional. Since the list is not all-inclusive, the teacher should feel free to add and delete as desired.

Phase I: Preparing for the Project

- Develop a vision of what the project will be and how it should look.
- Decide on sub-projects (pieces of the class project) for the students to build.
- Contact volunteers (if you decide to use them).
- Organize a flexible time schedule for the project.
- Collect resources and materials.
- Plan when you will need outside resource people, and contact them for a commitment. (Most will need plenty of advance notice.)
- Visit school and public libraries to see what resources are available.
- Collect folders of articles and pictures from the *National Geographic* and other sources.

Phase II: Beginning the Project

- Introduce the project and motivate the students.
- Plan geometry unit in math to coincide with figuring out buildings and the floor arrangement.
- Have students collect and bring in materials (cardboard, glue guns, etc.).
- Read aloud to the students from stories and/or books relating to the project.
- Get students working to put the map on the floor.

Phase III: Guiding the Project

- Actively move about the room assisting students with all phases of their work.
- Offer encouragement, guidance, and advice to anyone who needs it.
- Confer with and advise volunteers on a frequent basis.
- Periodically have class discussions that help students pull ideas together and make connections.
- Monitor supplies and building materials, and restock as necessary (cardboard, glue, paint, colored paper, etc.).
- Continue to read aloud to the students from stories and/or books relating to the project.
- Take pictures of construction in progress.

Phase IV: Culmination of the Project

- Prepare for Tour Day well in advance.
- Prepare and send invitations to parents.
- Arrange for publicity if appropriate.
- Arrange for refreshments and flowers.
- Arrange to have individual and groups projects labeled and all laid out ON TIME.
- Arrange for someone to take pictures of projects and events throughout Tour Day.

References

Bateson, Mary Catherine. 1989. *Composing a Life*. New York: Plume.

Bell, Terrel. 1991. Informal meeting with Idaho educators. Boise, ID.

Bloom, Benjamin S. 1956. *Taxonomy of Educational Objectives: The Classification of Educational Goals, Handbook I: Cognitive Domain*. New York: McKay.

Diamond, Marian C. 1988. *Enriching Heredity*. New York: The Free Press.

Dillard, Annie. 1987. *An American Childhood*. New York: Harper & Row.

Feynman, Richard P. 1985. *Surely You're Joking, Mr. Feynman*. New York: Bantam.

Gardner, Howard. 1985. *Frames of Mind*. New York: Basic Books.

———. 1991. *The Unschooled Mind*. New York: Basic Books.

Hooper, Judith, & Dick Teresi. 1986. *The 3–Pound Universe*. Los Angeles: Jeremy P. Tarcher.

Maxim, George W. 1991. *Social Studies and the Elementary School Child*. 4th ed. Columbus: Merrill Publishing Company.

McKibben, Bill. 1992. *The Age of Missing Information*. New York: Random House.

McLuhan, Marshall, & Quentin Fiore. 1967. *The Medium Is the Massage*. New York: Bantam.

Mittler, Gene A. 1989. *Art in Focus*. Columbus, OH: Glencoe Macmillan/McGraw-Hill.

Papert, Seymour. 1980. *Mindstorms*. New York: Basic Books.

Rheingold, Howard. 1988. *They Have a Word for It*. Los Angeles: Jeremy P. Tarcher.

Shekerjian, Denise. 1990. *Uncommon Genius*. New York: Viking.

Vygotsky, L.S. 1978. *Mind in Society*. Cambridge, MA: Harvard University Press.

Index

Also available from Heinemann. . .

History Workshop
Reconstructing the Past with Elementary Students
Karen L. Jorgensen
Foreword by **Yetta Goodman**

History Workshop is the first book to describe a process approach to history teaching that builds on children's natural curiosity about the past. Karen Jorgensen bases her work on the sociolinguistic premise that history learning is a language-thinking process in which children create historical meaning as they interact with others. In her book, she describes how children understand history and how she adapts the writing workshop approach to create a studio environment that encourages students to discover and rethink theories as they talk, read, write, and draw.
0-435-08900-5   1993   Paper

The Story of Ourselves
Teaching History Through Children's Literature
Edited by **Michael O. Tunnell** and **Richard Ammon**

In *The Story of Ourselves*, the contributors focus on the need for a history curriculum that is stimulating to students, with the application of children's trade book literature as an indispensable ingredient for such a curriculum. The book is a collection of writings by trade book authors and public school and college-level educators, designed to offer support and instruction for teachers who decide to use children's literature in their history/social studies programs. Contributing chapters to *The Story of Ourselves* are Newbery medalists Joan Blos and Russell Freedman, highly acclaimed authors Pam Conrad and Milton Meltzer, and artist Leonard Everett Fisher.
0-435-08725-8   1992   Paper

I've Got a Project On. . .
Geoff Ward

In this book, Geoff Ward explains how teachers can rethink the value of projects to ensure that children (and their parents) understand where these tasks fit in a curriculum, how they not only contribute to content learning but also help develop useful skills that will last through formal schooling and beyond.
PETA   0-90995-583-2   1989   Paper

These and other fine texts available through your local supplier or favorite bookstore.

Heinemann
361 Hanover Street
Portsmouth, NH 03801-3912
1-800-541-2086